Virtuous Pedophiles

Gary Gibson

DEDICATION

Virtuous Pedophiles is dedicated to people who find themselves sexually attracted to children but choose to not act on that attraction, with special thanks to all the virtuous pedophiles* whose comments contributed to this book. I also want to thank my wife, Tabitha Abel, who stood by me through all the drama.

Professionals who provide mental health services to people with pedophilia may appreciate this unique insight into the lives of non-offending pedophiles. Parents who are concerned that their son or daughter might be a pedophile may find this information invaluable. Partners of pedophiles may want to know if their loved one is at risk of sexually abusing a child. People with pedophilia will find hope and help in dealing with their unique sexual orientation.

The views expressed in this book may not always reflect the views of the founders or moderators of the forum by the same name (Virtuous Pedophiles), nor are the viewpoints expressed by other virtuous pedophiles necessarily held by this author.

*Pseudonyms in this book are indicated by an asterisk.

TRIGGER WARNING: *Virtuous Pedophiles* is written in simple but straightforward language meant for an adult audience. Discussion of sex has been a taboo topic in some circles. Any talk about pedophilia or child sexual abuse can arouse extreme emotions, so caution should be exercised in the reading of this book. Ignoring these subjects with silence will never resolve the myriad of problems connected with these two sides of the same coin. Secrecy is the friend of abuse. We need a fresh response to people with pedophilia that will help prevent child sexual abuse.

CONTENTS

WHAT IS A VIRTUOUS PEDOPHILE?

At first glance, the term "virtuous pedophile" appears to be an oxymoron. Many people conflate a pedophile with a child molester, and there is certainly nothing virtuous about molesting a child. If we want to have a rational discussion about a sensitive subject, we must come to some agreement regarding the meaning of the words we use. Webster (2017) defines a pedophile as "a person who is sexually attracted to children," while the American Psychiatric Association (APA, 2013) specifies prepubescent children "generally age 13 years or younger." Roget's Thesaurus (McCutcheon, 1998) includes several synonyms for the word *virtuous*, such as "celibate," "chaste" and "abstinent." Virtuous pedophiles recognize that they are sexually attracted to children but abstain from any sexual interaction with a child. They may also be referred to as non-offending pedophiles.

Americans generally spell it *pedophile* and pronounce it **ped**-uh-fahyl, while the British tend to spell it *paedophile* and say **pee**-dah-fahyl. Either way, is this the best term to use for a person who is sexually attracted to young children? Some prefer to use "minor attracted person" (MAP) in hopes that it will reduce the stigma surrounding pedophilia, just as the term "gay" was adopted by homosexuals.

Michael points out that the acronym MAP "came into existence with two express functions: (1) to adjust to the reality that the lay public and media alike have a nasty habit of misapplying chronophilic terminology ... and (2) to become more inclusive in our language in how we address the wider minor-attracted population."

One difficulty with the term MAP is that the definition of "minor" is so varied and the age of consent is arbitrary and subject to change. It dilutes the significance of the concept because most males are in fact sexually attracted to developed adolescents who are still minors. Such attraction is not a disorder.

Harry* writes, "I prefer to call a spade a spade and the word 'paedophile' is quite enough for me. It is loaded with associations, but I have enough tact to not use it when discussing my own stuff. If I had to choose an alternate label, I would go with Minor Attracted Person. I like how it states, very simply, what it is, but doesn't use gentle language to disguise itself. It communicates the point without having the unpleasant stigma of the proper word. I would argue that boy lover

(BL) and girl lover (GL) fail in this regard."

Scott* counters, "I'm not bothered by BL or GL or other terms as long as 'we' are using them. If you are part of that group, certain terms are OK and may not have the same connotation as if someone from the outside used them."

David* touches on an important principle, "BL and GL also seem a little off but I'm not going to tell other people how they should describe themselves."

Some mental health professionals use the expression "people with pedophilia" (PWP) because they consider it a mental disorder or at least a condition. Aaron* views it as a sexual orientation and considers it something he *is* rather than something he *has*. He observes, "I am trying to educate my current therapist about the viewpoint of pedophilia more as an orientation, and less as a disorder—assuming the latter can be cured via therapy."

Bobby* still favors talking about "having pedophilia." But whatever term you prefer, it is important to "use people-first language, and … not focus on the individual's disabling or chronic condition" (APA, 2010, p. 76).

VirPed Support Group

The internet has provided opportunities for people with pedophilia to interact anonymously. There are a number of online groups that do not take a stand against adult-child sex, such as B4U-ACT and Visions of Alice. Fred* points out one reason B4U-ACT took this approach. "To be fair, they only did that so as to avoid alienating pro-contact pedophiles who might need psychological help. They might be wrong, but they're not evil, and they have just as much right to be treated like human beings as everyone else."

Whatever personal views individual members may hold, B4U-ACT (2011) reminds participants that "minor-attracted people should abide by the law because of the potential risk to children and themselves of doing otherwise."

In June of 2012, two members, using the pseudonyms Ethan Edwards* and Nick Devin*, spun off a new support group called Virtuous Pedophiles (www.VirPed.org), which grew to more than 2,200 members in the first five years. In response to discussion about the name, Ethan* explains why VirPed chose the term pedophile rather than MAP. "There are a great many pedophiles who use 'MAP' trying to avoid the stigma of pedophilia…. We thought the main reaction to using 'MAP' would be 'You're just being devious and trying to hide with that term!'"

The group takes a strong stand against sexual interaction with a child, although Virtuous Pedophiles are not "perfect pedophiles." Convicted offenders are allowed to participate as long as they are committed to never abuse again. Sharing about non-adjudicated, illegal sexual activity is not allowed. Participants are not allowed to promote pro-contact views such as the legalization of adult-child sex. VirPed consists primarily of those who recognize they are sexually attracted to minors, plus some family members, research scientists, writers and journalists.

Those who join are usually comfortable saying something about themselves without revealing too much personal identifiable information. Abby* was surprised to find so many other females. "Hi, everyone! Didn't know there were so many women active here."

Trash* is typical of many new members, "Hey, I'm new around here, but not new to hating myself. My psychiatrist suggested I give this a shot so here I am. I am male, in my early 20s, AoA [age of attraction] 5-11 female, 18+ male. I experience depression, self-harm and self-hate."

Like most new members, Anton* was delighted to find VirPed. "It is nice to be in a forum of people who do *not* want to engage in sexual relationships with children. I have liked boys younger than me since I was 11 years old, and to this day I've never abused anyone, and never will."

Personally, I do not think of myself as a pedophile, but prefer to introduce myself with something like, "I have been sexually attracted to little girls for more than 60 years, but choose not to act on it. I am not exclusive and have been able to experience a fairly normal married life. I have three children and ten grandchildren."

Aydne* identifies himself as an offender. "I got off probation last month for a sex crime against a minor, and I'm sad to say it was partly because of not getting proper help with pedophilia. I tried to get help some time ago, it blew up in my face, and I isolated, kept it a secret, and here we are. I heard about Ender* from a news article.... didn't know there was a forum for this!"

Some have unique interests or fetishes. Ben* shares, "I have been somewhat attracted to young girls (and boys occasionally), especially when imagining them using the toilet (I guess it's the intimacy of the situation). I just need somewhere to talk about this, okay? I couldn't imagine ever saying anything about this to people I know and love. My parents would freak out."

Queer* writes, "I'm a nonbinary person in my 20's. I wouldn't say I have a primary attraction to children, so I'm not technically a pedophile, but I do have sexual thoughts about teens down to even babies. I identify as a pansexual quoiromantic androgyne, and I'm happy to talk about what that means."

New members often share how they discovered VirPed. Randy* says, "I found Virped through Ender Wiggin* with his inspiring tweets and articles on Medium.... I'm hoping that I can turn my bad luck of being born with pedophilia into a good cause to help protect children."

People join the forum for a variety of reasons.

Andy* explains, "I've joined this website cause I want to try to help people like us. I've struggled with my condition since I was 13, it's left me confused, depressed, angry and everything in between over the years, but now I've found myself on what feels like stable ground."

Psychstudent* is representative of the professional participants. "I am a forensic psychology student currently working towards my undergraduate degree. I have a special interest in paedophilia. My aim is to conduct my dissertation around the topic of paedophilia being a sexual orientation and not a deviance of mind.... At this stage I am simply trying to broaden my knowledge base and understanding."

Pedophile Profile

The profile of a pedophile as a homeless man wearing a trench coat and passing out candy to kids at the park in order to seduce a child into his white cargo van is rarely accurate. Wise parents who are concerned about protecting their children no longer focus on "stranger danger" or the registry of convicted sex offenders but realize that the greatest danger may be in their own home. Pedophiles are not monsters from another planet, although there are a few psychopathic pedophiles who do not care about what society thinks or the harm they cause to children. While many pedophiles do step over the line, the vast majority know it is wrong to have sexual contact with a child, do not want to harm children and have enough self-control to avoid abusing a child.

Virtuous pedophiles exist in all areas of society, oftentimes working with children, indistinguishable from other members of the community. There is no accurate profile of a pedophile, since they may look and act like anyone else. They are just as likely to be educated, employed, married and religious as any corresponding person in society at large (Abel & Harlow, 2001). A pedophile might be a pastor, teacher, coach, or any otherwise respectable citizen. In one large community study (n=8,718 males), 4.1% anonymously admitted that they had sexual fantasies involving children, of which 75.7% had never had any sexual contact with a child (Dombert & Schmidt et al., 2016). While statistics vary, it is clear that most pedophiles do not molest children.

Pedophilia: An *Attraction* to Children
Child Sexual Abuse: A Criminal *Action*

We must recognize the difference between attraction and action—between a pedophile and a child molester. We are not responsible for our attraction but we are accountable for our actions. The kind of people we find ourselves attracted to is not a matter of choice, but we can choose whether or not we will act on that attraction. While some people might actually choose to be gay, certainly nobody wakes up on their thirteenth birthday saying, "I want to be a pedophile." In most situations, people discover their sexual orientation sometime around puberty.

A pedophile is sexually attracted to children whether or not he or she has molested a child, whereas a child molester has sexually abused at least one child, whether or not he or she is sexually attracted to children. Heterosexuals know they are attracted to the opposite gender even before they become sexually active. Homosexuals are attracted to people of the same gender, yet most of them manifest self-control and are at no greater risk of raping anyone just because it may be difficult for them to find a sex partner. Those who have never met a virtuous pedophile may wrongly assume that anyone with pedophilia has already abused a child or is a ticking time bomb who will inevitably offend.

Lyrabelle* differentiates attraction from action. "I've never understood why defining 'sexual lifestyle' as unique from 'sexual orientation' was offensive to some people, especially some gay people. Doesn't saying they are the same thing negate the experiences of the many gay people who are married to heterosexual partners? Is a man less homosexual because he lives a heterosexual lifestyle? Personally, I don't think so. I know I'm not straight, even though I technically live a 'straight' lifestyle. Not differentiating between sexual orientation and sexual lifestyle erases the experiences of people for whom these two things are decidedly different."

Arousal happens somewhere between the attraction and action. Just as teleiophiles are not always sexually aroused by every adult they are attracted to, so pedophiles have some degree of control over their arousal patterns. We will deal with fantasies in a later chapter, where we discover that there is no consensus in this area.

Not All Pedophiles are Child Molesters

The majority of those who have a limited sexual interest in children will never abuse a child. A recent large (n=1,189) study of MAPs found that only 12.2% "had been convicted of either viewing child pornography or a sexual contact offense with a child aged 14 or younger" (Bailey, Hsu & Bernhard, 2016). Another study found that among those who have a preferential attraction to children, 75% have never had any sexual contact with a child (Dombert & Schmidt et al., 2016). Both anti-contact pedophiles (who believe that it is always wrong for an adult to sexually interact with a child) and pro-contact pedophiles (who would like to make it legal for an adult to have sex with a "willing" minor), are generally able to exercise enough self-control in order to live within the law and avoid molesting a child (Cash, 2016).

Not All Child Molesters are Pedophiles

"One review estimated that about 40 to 50 percent of adult sex offenders with child victims had pedophilic sexual interests (Seto, 2004)" (Butcher, Mineka, & Hooley, 2012, p. 485). More than half of those who molest children do not have pedophilia, but abuse a child for some other reason.

An important fact to consider is that "thirty to fifty percent of those who sexually abuse a child are children or adolescents themselves" (Tabachnick & Klein, 2011). A child's attraction to another child is not considered pedophilia.

Even though a person is not generally attracted to children, child sexual abuse may be perpetrated when the person is under the influence of an inhibition-reducing drug such as alcohol (Chamberlain, 2013).

Adults sometimes sexually abuse a child because they are not able to find an adult partner. Some people abuse a child because they are obsessed with power and control, rather than because they have a sex drive directed toward children. It is possible to sexually abuse a child even without any sexual interest or arousal. Child molesters who abuse for some reason other than pedophilia are often called situational offenders. In this book we focus on those who acknowledge that they are sexually attracted to children.

Pedophilia: Any Sexual *Interest* in Children

Virtually all human beings began their sexual journey with an attraction to another child, rather than an attraction to a fully developed adult. Most men continue to be attracted to developed teenagers who are still minors. The fifth edition of the Diagnostic and Statistical Manual of Mental Disorders does not include an attraction to older adolescents as a mental disorder. It specifically excludes from diagnosis "an individual in late adolescence involved in an ongoing sexual relationship with a 12- or 13-year-old" (APA, 2013, p. 697). However, statutory rape is an issue that should not be ignored.

Most people find that the age of those to whom they are attracted increases as they age, but people with pedophilia experience an ongoing attraction to children, generally of a certain age range and gender. They did not choose this orientation and apparently cannot change it any more than gay or straight people can change their sexual orientation.

It is difficult to determine what percent of the population are pedophiles because pedophilia appears on a spectrum from a minimal interest in a specific child to an exclusive attraction to children. The DSM-5 changed the name of the diagnosis to "pedophilic disorder," while continuing to use the general term "pedophilia" to describe any level of sexual interest in prepubescent children (APA, 2013). Ethan* points out that "there was no term before for a sexual interest in children that was not a disorder."

Sexual attraction to children is much more common than most of us would like to admit. In several studies that were conducted anonymously, up to "32% of community and college samples of men reported sexual attraction to children" (Hall, Hirschman & Oliver, 1995, p. 682). Another study found that one in four adult males acknowledge some sexual interest in children (Wortley, 2015). One British researcher concluded that "paedophiles fall within the normal distribution curve for human males ... [and] are more common than homosexuals" (Goode, 2010, p. 18).

Orientation: A Primary or Exclusive Attraction

"*Sexual orientation* refers to an enduring pattern of attraction, behavior, emotion, identity, and social contacts. The term *sexual orientation* should be used rather than *sexual preference*" (APA, 2010, p. 74). Although not all scientists agree, one researcher estimated that 10% of adult males experience pedophilia as a sexual orientation (Goode, 2010).

The printed edition of the DSM-5 states:

If they report an absence of feelings of guilt, shame, or anxiety about these impulses and are not functionally limited by their paraphilic impulses (according to self-report, objective assessment, or both), and their self-reported and legally recorded histories indicate that they have never acted on their impulses, then these individuals have a pedophilic sexual orientation but not pedophilic disorder (APA, 2013, p. 698).

Within six months after the release of the print edition, the American Psychiatric Association was pressured by members of the gay community to remove the word "orientation" and subsequently replaced it with the word "interest" in future online editions. Individuals who have a sexual interest in children but do not act on it and are not distressed by it are still excluded from a diagnosis of pedophilic *disorder*. We can conclude that at various levels, pedophilia may be viewed as an interest, an orientation or a disorder.

Historically, the expression "sexual orientation" came into use in the 1940s, when homosexuality was viewed as a disorder by most mental health professionals (MHP's). Homosexual relationships were illegal in most jurisdictions at that time. With the onset of the AIDS epidemic, men who were sexually active with other men were at greater risk of harm and death than those who were sexually involved with women, even though such a correlation did not necessarily indicate causation. The use of the term "sexual orientation" did not mean that acting on the attraction was acceptable, legal or harmless. Most scientists still recognize pedophilia as a sexual orientation in the sense that it is not chosen and there is no evidence that it can be eradicated.

In recent decades, many in the gay community have tried to distance themselves from pedophiles. Reasonable people recognize that there are some similarities, as well as differences between the two groups. Recognizing pedophilia as a sexual orientation will not diminish the rights of lesbian, gay or bisexual individuals or cause abuse of children to be legalized.

Pedophilic *Disorder*: Distress or Action

According to the DSM-5, three criteria are required for a diagnosis of pedophilic disorder:

A. Over a period of at least 6 months, recurrent, intense sexually arousing fantasies, sexual urges, or behaviors involving sexual activity with a prepubescent child or children (generally age 13 years or younger).

B. The individual has acted on these sexual urges, or the sexual urges or fantasies cause marked distress or interpersonal difficulty.

C. The individual is at least 16 years and at least 5 years older than the child or children in Criterion A. (APA, 2013, p. 697).

Using these criteria, "the highest possible prevalence for pedophilic disorder in the male population is approximately 3%-5%" (APA, 2013, p. 698). Therapists may at times seek to avoid giving a diagnosis of pedophilic disorder because people with pedophilia have become the most stigmatized pariahs in our society. Pedophilic disorder needs to be differentiated from other possible comorbid disorders such as antisocial personality disorder, substance abuse disorder and obsessive-compulsive disorder (APA, 2013).

Research indicating the prevalence of pedophilia at 1% to 2% of the population (Beier et al., 2009) is generally in reference to those who are *exclusively* attracted to children. Some professionals consider these the only "true" pedophiles. Therapists are expected to specify whether a client is exclusive or nonexclusive (APA, 2013).

There is little research involving female pedophiles, but the Child Molestation Prevention Study (Abel & Harlow, 2001) found that one in 3,300 women sexually abuse a child, while one in 20 men do so. Females are not as likely to be accused of abusing a child, even for the same behavior that would cause a male to be convicted. The number of those who abuse children may not be the same as the number who are sexually attracted to them, but all researchers agree that pedophilia is much more common among men than among women. However, female pedophiles may feel even more ostracized because there are so few of them. We recognize the significance of this population.

WHAT CAUSES PEDOPHILIA?

Most people with pedophilia wonder why they have an attraction they did not choose and cannot seem to change. Parents often want to know what caused their child to end up with an unusual sexual orientation. Nick* responds, "We all wonder why we are sexually attracted to kids, though in the end I suppose it doesn't really matter. The real key is to determine how to live with our attractions in a manner that allows us to lead happy, productive and law-abiding lives, and to avoid sexually interacting with children."

Just as scientists do not fully understand what causes a person to be gay, so they do not know whether pedophilia is genetic, caused by environmental factors or both.

Jay* suggests, "This is a natural and normal part of human sexuality." Most people would not describe pedophilia as normal, but of those who participated in a

VirPed poll, 62% indicated that they thought pedophilia was a natural variation.

Historians do not have a definitive answer regarding the origin of pedophilia, but throughout recorded history there have always been individuals who were sexually attracted to children. Pro-contact pedophiles may refer to pederasty in Greek culture as justification for sexual interaction with children today. In the ancient world, it was common for an older man to marry a barely pubescent girl. Christians must deal with the evidence that Mary gave birth to baby Jesus when she was an adolescent and married a man much older than herself. Until the past century, puberty was generally considered the dividing line between childhood and adulthood.

We will consider two major perspectives about the origin of sexuality that are held by various VirPed members.

Evolution and Sexuality

People with a worldview based on evolution typically believe that sex developed for the purpose of reproduction and evolved to include bonding and recreation. Ideas about sexual morality change with the times and are presently often based on consent and not causing harm. Current standards in society permit any type of sexual activity between consenting adults. Gay people can now marry in many jurisdictions, but sexual contact with a child is considered harmful because children are not mature enough to provide informed consent.

One challenge for the evolutionary viewpoint is, "What natural selection process was at work to cause some species (such as [chimpanze] bonobos) to develop pedophilic behavior?"

Todd concludes, "While some sex play may not be harmful to bonobo children, we know it can be, and often is, to human children. That, in this case, outweighs any considerations of its usefulness."

Larry* thinks "pedophilia has to have some biological and evolutionary purpose."

Ender* does not see any apparent adaptive evolutionary advantage for either pedophilia or homosexuality. "Wouldn't it be more advantageous if every member of the species could produce offspring?"

Andy* shares his opinion. "The real evolutionary benefit is the plasticity of human sexuality as a whole, a plasticity that allows for the variety of human sexuality that we see. It does seem likely that paedophilia isn't a discrete category but rather part of a continuum of age-preference, with most men being preferentially attracted to adolescents and young adults, fewer men being preferentially attracted to preteens or slightly older adults, and even fewer men being preferentially attracted to young children or much older adults."

Demetrius* adds, "Reproduction is not the only thing that makes an evolutionary trait positive, the only point of sex.... The purpose of sex can be for bonding, not just reproduction.... Sexual attraction can provide incentive to bond, help, or protect someone else."

Ethan* says, "The simplest explanation is that it's just a mistake in the wiring with no adaptive function.... If it was adaptive, why wouldn't it be adaptive for all?"

Nick* has the final word. "Better to stick with what you know, and not speculate about things that you don't know."

Creation and Sexuality

On the other hand, people who subscribe to Intelligent Design believe that God invented sex—for the preservation of the species, as well as mutual satisfaction. Christians who base their religion on the Bible maintain that the ideal sex is between one man and one woman, who willingly enter into a lifetime commitment to an exclusive intimate relationship. Gay people might be treated with respect, while homosexual practices are condemned; just as people with pedophilia may be tolerated, but any sexual contact with a child is considered a grievous sin.

One challenge with this worldview is, "Why did God make me a pedophile?" Magnus* explains, "I think God wanted me to be a pedophile ... because the emotional side of my attraction makes me want to protect children."

Greenwood* proposes another perspective. "This world isn't as God originally made it. People are distant from God, and so is creation. There are natural disasters and disease. Pedophilia is just one of the many conditions that affect humans. However, God's plan is to be a part of each person's life, whoever will accept Him. He was Jesus when He came to earth, and now He will be with each person spiritually. God's goal is to help us have victory."

Another challenge for those who believe in God is the desire to "pray the gay away," or in this case attempt to "pray the pedophilia away." Personally I am not helped by those who tell me I just need to pray more. I have prayed about it for sixty years, but so far God has not chosen to remove that temptation from me.

Nature vs. Nurture: Heredity or Environment

Scientists do not know exactly what causes pedophilia, but preliminary research using *f*MRI brain scans of convicted offenders found that pedophilic sexual offenders were more likely to be shorter, non-right-handed and have a lower IQ than non-sexual offenders (Cantor et al., 2004). These factors have genetic markers, which tend to indicate that pedophilia may have some hereditary component. The research does not suggest that all pedophiles are left-handed or that all left-handed people are pedophiles. It does not indicate anything about the intelligence of individuals, whether non-offending pedophiles or non-pedophiles. More recent research revealed a difference in the white brain matter of inmates who were sexually attracted to children compared with those who were not, which these researchers describe as a cross wiring between sexuality and the nurturing instinct for children (Cantor & Blanchard, 2012).

Afuche* suggests a possible combination. "I view atypical sexual orientations and attractions as a combination of a natural susceptibility and triggering events that happen during childhood or adolescence. So people without the natural susceptibility who experienced potentially triggering events and people with the natural susceptibility who did not experience triggering events would remain heterosexual teliophiles. But for people who are both naturally susceptible and experienced triggering events, that combination would affect and change their sexual orientation and attractions."

Eric* adds, "I think the twig was already bent toward pedophilia before I was born, but then there were certain incidents and curiosities throughout my childhood that made me grow into a pedophile ... well on my way by age 8, and fully formed by 15 or 16."

In my own experience, my maternal grandfather

sexually abused my mother and her sister. My paternal grandmother sexually abused my father and his brother. My father sexually abused several of my sisters. Whatever predisposition I may have inherited was apparently initialized by typical sex play when I was young. At the age of six, my older sisters taught me to play "go to sleep," which meant I was to take their panties off and get them ready for bed. Although I do not consider it abuse, it left me with the distinct impression that girls want to have boys touch them. Then when I was twelve, my older male cousin taught me to play "doctor" with his younger sisters, which involved checking out their private parts.

Experiencing childhood sexual abuse appears to have some correlation with becoming an abuser but is neither a necessary nor a sufficient condition to cause pedophilia (Jespersen, Lalumiere & Seto, 2009).

Other people with pedophilia identify their early access to pornography as being a contributing factor, although many boys and girls have similar experiences without developing pedophilia.

Nedley* adds another interesting perspective. "I'm not saying all autistics are pedophiles or vice versa. I said *in my case*. I believe the developmental delay and arrest in my sexual development left me stuck at the developmental level of a 10-12 year old sexually." Indeed, a surprising number of Virtuous Pedophiles are also autistic.

Demetrius* writes, "As far as prepubescents go, I'd

say it's no different than a preference for any other body type…. It just happens to be one of the least popular preferences."

"There isn't one cause of paedophilia," Peter* concludes. "Various forms of paedophilia might in each case be something arrived at by a final common pathway."

What is Pedophilia?

The choice of language used in discussing this subject is influenced by how one looks at pedophilia. Which is it?

A disorder or a sexual orientation?

Normal or abnormal?

Learned or inherited?

Natural or unnatural?

Innate or acquired?

Immutable or changeable?

An addiction or an obsession?

Pedophilia is clearly not a choice, nor is it a crime as long as one does not act on it; but there is rarely a consensus about some of the other attributes. Professionals recognize that it can be both a sexual orientation and a mental illness at the same time (APA, 2013). Perhaps it is a bit of both nature and nurture, with both hereditary and acquired components.

Anton* writes, "I honestly believe my condition is both a disorder and sexual orientation. I really like the idea that in the absence of guilt, shame and anxiety then pedophilia is not a mental illness."

Sagit* informs us that pedophilia is "presented in SOTP [sex offender treatment programs] as a 'condition,' 'sickness' or 'compulsive disorder.' It is none of the above. It is a sexual orientation. It is intrinsic, unchangeable, immutable."

Nick* adds, "I did not choose my sexual orientation, and there is nothing I can do to change it. I cannot be evil simply because I have sexual feelings that I didn't choose and can't change."

Craig* hints at a possible genetic link. "I tend to think that there's some biological component involved. But usually our sexual attractions and orientation become more apparent at puberty."

Bean* expresses the same thought. "Though it may not be as simple as born with a given gene, it is not an active or conscious choice one makes to be attracted to someone. I'm bi myself and believe it to be due to a confluence of childhood experiences, potential biological predispositions, and addiction, but who knows."

Whenever comments are allowed in a public discussion of this subject, someone will suggest a bullet in the head as the solution for pedophilia. A certain element of society has always used inhumane treatment on people they hate. "Kill them all" was the cry against Jews in Nazi Germany. "Castrate them" was at one time forced on Black people in the United States (Schmidt, 1983). Some people hoped the gay community would self-destruct with the AIDS epidemic. Are any of these viable solutions for people with pedophilia? Even if we could "banish them all to a deserted island," more would be born. How would you respond if it were your son or your daughter?

Undoubtedly, researchers will continue to seek for the cause of pedophilia in hopes of curing it. Many of us who ended up with this unique sexual orientation that we did not choose and apparently cannot change, realize that we are responsible for what we do with it. Whether it is caused by nature or nurture, heredity or our environment, whether it is genetic or acquired, we will probably have to deal with it throughout our lifetime. The most important thing we need to know is that abuse of children is not inevitable nor acceptable.

With most diseases, scientists look for the cause in hopes of finding a cure. If pedophilia is strictly inherited, we would expect it to be bred out, as prepubescent children (the target of the attraction) do not generally produce offspring. If child sexual abuse is the primary cause, we would expect a lot more females than males to become pedophiles. For those who view pedophilia as a sexual orientation, the bad news is, there is no cure. The good news is that pedophilia can be managed effectively so that the person can live a meaningful, law-abiding life.

COMING OUT OF THE TOY BOX

Someone adapted the expression "coming out of the closet" from the gay community and suggested that people with pedophilia come out of the "toy box." Prior to making such an acknowledgment to someone else, one must first become conscious of his or her own sexual orientation. This awareness usually occurs sometime around puberty.

Personally, I became aware that I was sexually attracted to little girls when, at the age of 12, I played "doctor" with my older male and younger female cousins. I thought it was wrong but it did not seem abnormal to me at the time because every male I knew appeared to be sexually interested in young girls. Stories of child sexual abuse were common, not only in my family of origin but in many other families I knew.

Fortunately, I am not exclusive and am also attracted to adult women. I am married with three children and ten grandchildren, which I determined I would never abuse. My pedophilia simmered in the background for the 25 years of my first marriage. I spent a lot of time around children and even taught school for a number of years. With every story of abuse, I saw myself as a potential child abuser, even though I was determined not to cause a child the harm that five of my older siblings had experienced. I internalized the hatred so often expressed against people with pedophilia, but still did not think of myself as a pedophile.

When I found myself single again in the late nineties, I spent some time in the South Pacific, where young children often run around naked. But for the grace of God and my own self-control, I might have initiated sexual contact with one of the girls. When I returned to the United States, I told my counselor that I was struggling with an attraction to little girls. She was shocked and said she could not deal with it. She promptly abandoned me without a referral, leaving me feeling even more vulnerable, helpless and hopeless.

Self-Awareness

People with pedophilia describe a variety of experiences in coming to the realization that they are attracted to young children. Craig* figured it was an occasional quirk. "I just thought of myself as having normal attractions, with this sometimes unexplainable thing for a girl who was too young for me. That's exactly the way I put it to myself—not a 'little girl,' just someone who was a bit (or quite a bit) too young still."

Max* has vivid memories of his first realization. "The moment it hit me like a ton of bricks was beginning on July 20th 2004. This day or the day before I had played with three girls aged 6-8 on the beach of the Baltic Sea and those three girls were naked all the time. We built sandcastles together and at some point two of the girls knelt down to take sand and doing this they spread their legs towards me."

Andy* also recalls when it happened. "I remember the exact moment my sexuality properly woke up, so to speak. I was nine years old, and these two girls who were walking in front of me suddenly seemed utterly gorgeous."

BS* cannot remember any particular moment that he became aware of his attraction to young boys. "It was always gradual and slow in a way. I have evidences of it maybe since I was as young as seven, some others at the age of eight, and since I was 12 I was checking pictures of boys in underwear and naked boys. Also I wanted to check boys out at camps and stuff since I was 12."

On the other hand, Ethan* says it took years for him to admit it. "My strongest attraction is to girls as young as four. I'm also attracted to older females, though the attraction drops off sharply above age 30. I'm very fortunate in this regard, because I've been able to form loving relationships with adult women. This wider range of attraction also let me deny the reality of my pedophilia until I was about 50."

Consequences of Coming Out

After I remarried, my wife and I built a home and took care of three foster children in 2007. She wonders why I did not object and come out to her at that time, but I had been around children and managed my attraction for many years so I did not expect it to be a problem. Besides, it is very embarrassing to admit you are a pedophile, even to someone who really loves you. After a few months, the children were returned to their homes and we moved on to other projects.

Two days before Christmas in 2010, the state police questioned me, claiming that the girl who had been ten when she was with us alleged that I had molested her. I knew the "memories" that she developed years after leaving our home were false and offered to take a polygraph test, although later I declined on the advice of an attorney. The allegations were dismissed because of the lack of evidence. Even though no charges were filed, the only hospital in our county banned me from their premises for about two years.

The experience gave me the courage to come out to my wife, as well as my sisters, children and many other relatives. My wife encouraged me to become a licensed professional counselor so that I could help other people with pedophilia before they acted on their attraction. When I had nearly completed a master's degree in mental health counseling, I was dismissed from the university based solely on my sexual orientation, which set me free from being a mandatory reporter.

By that time I had become active as a member of the Association for the Treatment of Sexual Abusers. I became acquainted with many professionals from around the world. Gene Abel was the first one to give me confidence that I would never abuse a child. Klaus Beier from the German Prevention Project Dunkelfeld inspired me to envision something similar in the United States. I became acquainted with and learned to respect professionals in the field such as James Cantor, David Finkelhor, Joan Tabachnick, Michael Seto, Elizabeth Letourneau and David Prescott.

I began participating in three online support forums for minor attracted persons. Like others, I used a pseudonym at first, but eventually decided to use my real name and contact information. I was open about the fact that I am a Christian and opposed to any sexual interaction between an adult and a child. I do not impose my values on others, so gradually people on the forums gained confidence in me and began to contact me for additional support. Over the past few years I have provided referrals to MHPs for dozens of those who feel the need for in-person therapy.

My wife and I founded the Association for Sexual

Abuse Prevention (ASAP) in 2015. We held workshops to help professionals understand the best ways of responding to non-offending pedophiles. I also made numerous presentations to students studying sexuality at a university.

In 2014 I participated in a live Oregon Public Broadcasting talk show without any negative repercussions, so early in 2017 I agreed to be interviewed by The Sun (a tabloid in the UK), not realizing the dire consequences it would have. About the same time, someone posted (with my permission) a YouTube video of me telling my story at an ASAP workshop. This information got circulated in our local community and created quite a stir, with even a few death threats.

In one week of January 2017, my wife and I shared our story on four live television and radio talk-shows. The next week Dr. Phil invited us to appear on his show. We agreed. Overall we got a positive response, as thinking people realized we were helping prevent child sexual abuse. Some responded with the typical pedophilia hysteria, but true friends did not abandon us.

Women who had been sexually abused as children were often supportive because they wished someone had been there to prevent their abuse from happening. Men who had become abusers told us they wished someone had been there to help prevent them from becoming molesters. Some professionals saw us as heroes who were breaking ground in this field and our gay friends were supportive because they had experienced similar stigma and understood that we were not trying to destigmatize child sexual abuse. Our family and friends "got it" because they understood the difference between attraction and action. Most of them did not treat me any differently from before I came out of the toy box and still allowed me to be around their children. I do regret the embarrassment that some of them experienced because of my coming out so publicly, even though it has been helpful to many other people.

We were disappointed that our local church and statewide church organization immediately banished both my wife and I without following Biblical principles or church policy. Hopefully they will come to realize that such actions do nothing to protect children and merely drive the problem underground.

Be Cautious Coming Out

Unfortunately, John* was also mistreated when he came out of the toy box to ask for help, "The guy I went to was allegedly someone who was trained to deal with this issue. I told him that I had been having certain fantasies about my step-daughter. After a couple of sessions he decided that he had to report these things to DCFS [Department of Child and Family Services] even though I hadn't acted on any of them.

"A social worker and sheriff deputy showed up at

my door at dinner time. I was forced to move out of my house that night, for as long as the investigation took…. After speaking to some of my other therapists, DCFS was satisfied that I had only revealed fantasies, not actions. In the end, they shared with me that they felt the therapist had been trigger happy and had reported unnecessarily.

"But that wasn't the end of it. They put our family under a six month visitation schedule. For those six months, I was not allowed to be alone with either of my step-children, even the boy who holds no sexual interest for me. They came by every couple of weeks and interviewed the children. It was awful. This came from seeing a therapist who was supposedly one of the few out there specifically trained to deal with this issue! It is my opinion that there is no 'safe' form of therapy for a pedophile who is trying not to act out. My seeking therapy was to ensure that everyone in my home remained safe, especially my step-daughter. It blew up in my face. I will never seek professional help again, because I just don't trust the system."

Crystal* sought help while in the air force. She was stigmatized as a criminal and discharged even though she never had any sexual contact with a child. "I've not had very good luck when it comes to therapy. My first [therapist] outed me and the next two made feel like a sociopath. I even had one tell me that I was faking my attractions and only men suffer from pedophilia."

Glen* shares the trauma he experienced in coming

out. "I was super stressed due to changing my medications and feeling like I might act out on some of my urges towards children. I naively went to the mental health place at the hospital and told them what I was worried about. When I first showed up they were friendly and seemed like they wanted to help. All they did was call the police and offered absolutely zero support."

Dale* reports, "The first therapist I had immediately contacted Child Protective Services. They proceeded to contact all of my friends and family with prepubescent girls, which led to me being ostracized. This eventually led to a suicide attempt which almost succeeded."

Adam expresses his disappointment, "I've had so many bad experiences with MHPs, I'm not sure I trust them. I have come across people who tried to pretend that minor attraction does not exist. According to them, I am not a reliable witness of my own sexuality. According to them, I am too intelligent, too good looking, and too socially competent to be minor attracted. According to them, I am also confused; I am not minor attracted, I only think that I am."

Jay* shares his experience when he outed himself after being on an emergency hold for suicidal ideation. "At the state hospital, I was told I belong in prison and that if I did kill myself I would be doing society a favor. The greatest part about being told this is that it was by my patient advocate."

Coming Out Can Be Therapeutic

It is easier to come out anonymously, even though many who join VirPed say it is still very difficult to write those words for the first time. Alan* reached out in the darkness. "This may be the hardest thing I've ever had to write. I am a 28 year old man and I have an attraction to boys aged about 8 upwards."

It may be frightening, but Slade* claims it gets better quickly. "Hey everyone. I just wanted to say how amazing this place is. For the longest time I thought I was alone. I'm in my very early 20's and am glad this place exists. I've been a member for 5 minutes and I feel 90 times better."

Jared* describes how VirPed helped. "I have 'come out' as a boy lover. It happened right here on VirPed and I can't thank you guys enough for allowing what many people in the LBGT community already have the luxury of doing. We don't. We may never experience what it would be like to tell the whole world that we have a sexual preference towards children and that we are happy and OK about it. But my life has changed and for the better. I work with children and I have developed some beautiful close friendships with mostly boys, but a few girls too. Watching them grow up and become successful as adults feels so good. Many of them keep in touch with me and credit me for their success in music."

No single support group can meet everyone's

needs. In describing his experience with VirPed, Bean* wrote, "VirPed served a great purpose at a specific time in my life. I no longer feel that being active on here is necessary or even desired, though I may still pop in from time to time. It helped me to find myself, and amazing things have happened in my life as of late. I went from having little hope to now having a special someone in my life who I hope to someday marry and have kids with. I used to think it was impossible, and I can only attribute it to a miracle of God that I found this person in my life."

The founders encourage caution in coming out, even though many have found it to be a positive experience. Nick* describes what happened when he finally went to see a therapist. "I did a lot of research, so I was reasonably confident he'd be sympathetic, but still, talking to him was the most terrifying thing I've ever done. I must have talked nonstop for a half an hour. When I finished, he just smiled and said, 'You know, being sexually attracted to children doesn't make you a bad person if you don't have sex with them. After all, you didn't choose to be sexually attracted to children and you can't stop being sexually attracted to children, but you can and have successfully resisted your attraction. That makes you a good person, not a bad person, and I admire you for that.'"

Guy* writes, "It makes me feel really good knowing that I've come out to so many people and they somehow still respect me. I can't imagine it's easy hearing that someone so close to you can't help but sexualize children, in my opinion. Yet they still respect me, and some even more since I have no problem abstaining, considering my … teenage sex drive."

Mario* describes a good experience coming out to his youth pastor. "He told me that although he doesn't understand it he knows that what I struggle with towards children isn't any different from my struggle with women or his struggle with women…. I have helped work with our youth ministry doing the rather usual tasks that are behind the scenes…. He trusted me to not take advantage of anything, which is true of me."

Things to Consider before Coming Out

- Identify the reasons why you want to come out.
- Evaluate how trustworthy the person is.
- Consider the impact it will have on the person you tell and others who find out.
- Consider the impact it will have on you if they out you to someone else.
- Be willing to accept whatever response you get.

PEDOPHILE IN THE HOUSE

"My partner is a pedophile!" Dominick* cried out in desperation. "I don't know how to broach the subject with anyone, because most people can't fathom that a woman might be a pedophile. She definitely does not want anyone to know."

He described how they met at a wedding, where he was horrified to hear a group of people talking about abusing children. At the time, he did not realize his new girlfriend had any connection with that group. She was a little older than he and pursued him. In spite of insisting that she was infertile, she became pregnant when they had only dated for one month. "Now a year later we have a newborn baby together, but the majority of her friends are active pedophiles, who have sex with children, film it, and sell it."

He explained why he believes his baby girl is at risk. "One of these 'friends' came from Belgium with her daughter to meet us. My partner took me to a flat right next to a school with this friend, where they organized the details of when they were going to put our daughter in 'movies.' I don't know what to do….

"I have been tricked into having a child for a pedophile gang so they can use my daughter as some sort of disposable abuse victim. What's even worse is I'm so alone. I tried to tell my parents, but they don't believe me and think I'm making it up. They made me see a doctor, who diagnosed this as a delusion and had me committed. In the mental health ward I was told that this was a paranoid delusion, that it was not true. I reported it to a police officer, a doctor, and the mental health professionals, none of whom did anything. It is difficult since my partner is female and I have no solid evidence of any of this. I honestly don't know what to do. Please help me, as you're my last and only hope!"

How Best to Respond

Perhaps this man is delusional, but what would you do if someone you love came out of the toy box to you? How would you respond if you discovered that your father or mother, husband or wife, sister or brother, son or daughter was sexually attracted to children? Who could you turn to for help if your teenager realized that the age of those he or she is attracted to does not increase as they get older? It takes a lot of courage to seek help in such a serious situation. If you are an

MHP, how would you respond if a client recognizes he or she is sexually attracted to children but has never acted on it? People with pedophilia should be able to seek help from a therapist, but it is not easy to find anyone who has experience in dealing with non-offending pedophiles. A recent study found that 95% of licensed professionals do not want to treat people with pedophilia (Cacciatori, 2017). One purpose of this book is to change the way we respond to this population so that it will be safe for a non-offending pedophile to seek professional help.

There are some fair questions that need to be addressed. Has the pedophile molested a child or viewed pornography involving children? Are children really at risk of being harmed by this person? Should I call the authorities? If you are not a mandatory reporter, it may be best to wait for the answer to these questions until you have looked at the bigger picture. If this loved one has voluntarily come out to you, it will not be helpful to assume that they have molested a child or are a monster waiting to abuse a child.

Reporting active abuse might prevent the abuse from continuing, but in the long run there is no evidence that mandatory reporting laws actually protect children. They have been found to be counter-productive. "The number of self-referrals for child abuse and the self-disclosure rate during therapy both went to zero, and the number of children identified as abused did not increase" (Zuckerman, 2008, p. 390).

However, there is evidence that we have pushed child sexual abuse even further underground.

Experience of Family Members

Mozel* is the kind of parent that every pedophile would love to have. "I am the mother of an adult homosexual son in his late 30s, who told me about his pedophilic orientation about a half year ago. I've known about his homosexuality since he was sixteen. He is and will always be my beloved son. I ache for whatever he has suffered and may still suffer. I hope he will someday find a partner with whom to share his life. Despite everything, he has already made and will continue to make a happy life for himself, full of friends and family who love and adore him. He urged me to understand more about the challenges that face him and the parents of other pedophiles."

A ConcernedWife* explains her reason for coming to VirPed. "My husband recently disclosed that he is attracted to pre-pubescent girls. I felt like I was drowning and he had handed me a dump truck. It seemed to come out of nowhere; I didn't have any idea. After the initial shock wore off, I came to realize I was actually okay with it."

Rose* reports a similar experience. "My husband came out to me while we were on date night. I had no idea about the significance or type of attraction he had, as he himself was still working it out. I've noticed there are a few stages to it. First there's a time of receiving it, digesting it, and understanding it. Then there comes the stage of trying to deal with it, keeping everyone as healthy and happy as they can be without doing anything illegal. As a family unit, that is very important. Right now I'm still in the stage of trying to keep support going for my husband and am currently reaching out to see if there is more that I can do for him. I have lots of feelings and emotions, depending on the issues at hand and how difficult it is for my husband to deal with what he is going through."

Fran* describes how difficult it can be. "I'm the wife of one of the members here, and I'm still trying to cope. I don't know how to handle it. We have children which fall into his age and gender of attraction. Unlike most others here, he does not seem to find them entirely sexually unappealing. He's getting help from mental health experts, and he's not been alone with the children, so I'm fully confident that he's telling the truth, and nothing has ever happened, but that's a hard thing to deal with!"

ConcernedWife* commiserates, "I find it reassuring that I can ask my husband anything and he answers honestly. No matter how awkward or embarrassing or difficult. It's the only reason I'm still with him. I have made it abundantly clear that the kids are my priority so he needs to be open and accountable."

Anton* identifies himself as a partner to a pedophile who was convicted of a sexual offense and explains his reason for joining VirPed. "In Sweden where we live, Pat* gets all sorts of help from society, but as a relative there is *no* help. This is my channel for my worries and questions, to read, write and ask. It was Pat* that introduced me here this spring. This is just a place for me to be open about the fact that I actually have a relationship with a pedo."

Yuki* sought out the VirPed forum to learn how to help her husband. "I am trying to support my husband. I know he is a pedophile, but I don't think he knows I know. I want to let him know that I know and urge him to get into counseling or something to make sure he stays on the right path. I'm making this post specifically to ask for some feedback on a few of my ideas and then also to see if there are any specific actions you might suggest I take or *not* take:

"1. Do you think it's possible he's looking at child pornography because he isn't getting what he needs from me?"

If he is looking at child pornography, it is not her fault. ConcernedWife* advises, "He's an adult making his own decisions. Forcing yourself to have more sex when you don't want to will probably not have the desired outcome."

"2. Would limiting his internet access be helpful?" Yuki* continues.

ConcernedWife* replies, "I don't believe in

parenting my husband. I would limit it only if he requested it, but the onus would still remain on him to learn to control himself."

"3. Has sharing a secret about yourself helped your effort to connect with and support your friend or family member?" Yuki* queries.

ConcernedWife* agrees, "Yes. My husband only came out to me because I shared a large chunk of my past with him. It was the only reason he felt safe saying something. Because I was open, vulnerable and willing to answer anything he asked, he felt he needed to be as open and honest."

"4. Does role-playing help or do you think it drives a person to want to 'do the real thing' more?" Yuki* concluded her questioning for the moment.

Some Virtuous Pedophiles would avoid role-playing, while others find it helpful in decreasing the risk that they might act out with a real child. This kind of peer support has been helpful to both people with pedophilia and family members.

Do not despair if you learn that your child or some other loved one has pedophilia. He or she will appreciate your support rather than condemnation.

First, learn all you can about the subject. "Pedophilia per se appears to be a lifelong condition. Pedophilic disorder, however, necessarily includes other elements that may change over time with or without treatment" (APA, 2013, p. 699). The attraction or orientation does not change, but treatment can modify arousal patterns and reduce the "subjective distress" and the "propensity to act out sexually with children." There is hope.

Opportunity for a Deeper Relationship

Some people are satisfied with a superficial relationship, but if someone you love has chosen to come out to you with this secret part of themselves, consider it an opportunity to develop a deeper relationship.

ConcernedWife* writes, "I do believe being honest with a spouse or potential spouse is important. Hiding something like this has the potential to create issues that can be hurtful when only one person knows what is really going on. Being married for so long and then finding out is a whole different ball game then having that discussion at the onset. I do understand the words of caution the members who are more experienced have shared. It is not a decision to take lightly, but neither is getting married."

On the other hand, Nick* does not feel it is necessary to come out to your spouse. "I've been married for a long time and I've never said a word about it. For some reason it has never bothered me. I know there are others on the site who feel that way as well. My view is that my wife and I are both very happy.

Saying something would risk both our happiness and would help no one."

Eustace* says, "I told my wife about my behaviors related to attraction to boys before we got married. It took a while after we got married for me to talk more deeply with her about my feelings. I think she deserved to know, and that took priority over my worries about how she would respond."

Mara* thinks that if she liked a guy enough that he might become her hubby, she would "feed him with the information about my mental health and sexuality in small, lukewarm, sugarcoated chunks."

Brad* shares a good experience coming out to his girlfriend. "I'm honestly shocked that I felt comfortable telling her so soon, considering I've only known her for just over two weeks. But I started probing for how she thought about the ethics of sex and attraction in general, trying to guess at how she'd react, and I decided that she'd probably be OK with it. And I was right! Besides, I figured that if she was going to dump me over this, it would be best to find out early."

Minky* urges caution about sharing with someone that might not remain your friend. "Always remember that a girlfriend might become an ex-girlfriend and it's super important to know her true character. My one ex-girlfriend knows and I regret that. She hates me, so she obviously isn't a person who I would share this info with now."

Susan* adds, "Even though it's still incredibly hard

for me to even say the word 'pedophile' out loud, I feel like it's probably easier being a woman and coming out to a male partner. Honestly, though, find another pedophile, or someone who is willing to be open with discussions about sexuality! I could never go back to keeping it a shameful secret. It affects how I see myself to feel the need to hide it all the time."

Sweetie* writes, "I dated a man and about six months in he told me he was attracted to very young girls. He didn't really know what answer to expect from me, but he definitely did not expect me to say 'me too.'"

Stan* was surprised by his father's response. "I trusted my dad enough to tell him I was a pedophile, even if the idea made me sick…. He just said, 'Well, alright. You're a pedophile. How young?' I said I was attracted to girls 4 years old or up. In a satisfied tone he said, 'Okay. You feel better?' … He said that he was so sorry that I had to grow up sexually repressed to the point where just a sexual attraction brought me so much pain and sadness and that it shouldn't have, even if it was a sensitive one such as this."

My wife has had her own journey. "I had never met anyone who was sexually attracted to children," she said, "when Gary first told me this. His persona did not match what I assumed were the evil, dirty pedophiles I had seen on the TV. Some, admittedly had the exterior of being great people with a strong desire to help kids – and had gone off the rails, somehow. Others were disgusting in my sight, but I had no idea that it was so difficult for them to get help *before* they acted on that attraction. Then I did not know that the ugly mug-shots were of people who had already molested a child and may, or may not be pedophiles even though they were given that title by ignorant people.

"But could I believe he had never acted on that attraction? I had to go on who I knew him to be –but no one can know 100% that someone is telling the truth. I do believe him, and stating that publicly has resulted in people sending me hate mail, wanting to kill me and saying that I am as bad as him. For my part I believe I am married to a very bold man who has knowingly publicly admitted his sexual attraction, not action, and put his life (and mine) at risk of death because he wants to make the world a safer place one child at a time, and wants to help others like him get professional help before they go down the desperate path to molestation, depression and or suicide. Not everyone is willing to go on the record, but the price is high. Hatred is palpable at times and yet all know that life isn't fair and I am not responsible for other peoples' words or actions. God, I believe, is in control and gives me opportunities to work for two populations (pedophiles and children) that have no voice. It is a gift, an unwanted gift, but I chose to stand with Gary."

VirPed has a special section for "partners of pedophiles" and someone recently offered to start a separate forum specifically for them.

How You Can Help

Pedophilia appears on a broad spectrum from those who experience an occasional or minimal sexual attraction to children to those who are exclusively attracted to children. Nick* encourages those who are not exclusively attracted to children to focus on their adult relationships. Many of us are happily married. You might be able to help a person with pedophilia develop and maintain a romantic relationship with another adult.

But is it possible for an exclusive pedophile to develop a satisfying relationship with an adult? Ender* learned to love a woman. "I am exclusively attracted to boys, and yet I am married and have a satisfactory sexual life with my wife.... I fully believe you can indeed learn to love a woman. Of course, there is no guarantee that it will ever happen, and I realize how lucky I was and that it won't happen to everyone, but it is possible."

Anton* agrees. "It´s possible to have an adult relationship. I´m partner with Pat,* an exclusive boylover and what we have is very special. I love this man dearly and he is my family. I have during our year together reached the possibility that he might never love me in the same way I love him. But what we have is so special. We found each other in a time where we both were weak and our affection for each other has only grown since…. Yes, it's possible to have an adult relationship, even if it could be a bumpy road."

Some who for religious or other reasons are opposed to homosexual relationships still recognize that developing an adult homosexual relationship is better than risking the possible abuse of a child. While Virtuous Pedophiles is not a dating site, there are a number of couples who have gotten together after meeting on the forum. One of these couples recently had a baby.

Not all pedophiles need to be prevented from being around children. Many find that being around groups of children actually helps reduce any risk that they might act out with a child. After an evaluation of the risk factors, you may be able to provide support as a prevention partner when the person with pedophilia does interact with children.

Art* believes that "for most pedophiles time spent in a safe space working with kids voluntarily could be helpful for us. It is incredibly rewarding for me to spend time with and help them."

Ernie* agrees that it can be helpful to spend time with children with others present. "I found that the more time I spent around my little sister with my dad or step-mom present and being in the vicinity of her and other children in public settings, the more I came to see them as real human beings with their own feelings, thoughts, and personalities rather than sex objects."

Sandy* says his "capacity to resist temptation is a

bit like a muscle. Mine hasn't atrophied through decades of avoiding contact with children. And being in contact with children regularly ensures they are never dehumanized and rendered an abstraction, with considerations about how to behave around them becoming merely theoretical."

Children have always been an important part of my life. The support of my wife and other family members has been helpful in maintaining appropriate boundaries with children.

Last but not least, if you are spiritually inclined, pray with and for your pedophile friend.

ASSESSING THE RISK

While there is some risk that any living human being could sexually interact with a child, there is no crystal ball that can determine exactly who will become a child molester. Even those professionals who realize that most people with pedophilia are not seeking out children to abuse, still consider pedophiles to be at a higher risk of offending than those who have no sexual attraction to children. Therapy will often emphasize the development of a safety plan to manage urges. This approach is not always appreciated by or necessary for non-offending pedophiles.

Art* does not feel he is at any risk. "I don't have strategies to not offend. I don't have urges either. I really hate the word."

Craig* maintains, "I can't say I've ever had urges to offend that are difficult to resist."

Peter* doesn't want to be praised for not acting on his urges. "Many pedophiles can control their urges and not rape children just as any normal, heterosexual male can be attracted to a woman, control his sexual urges and not rape her."

Personally, I am sexually attracted to little girls but generally don't get aroused or have overwhelming urges to have sexual contact with them. I feel more vulnerable when I have developed an ongoing friendship with a girl I find attractive, and therefore I simply avoid being alone with her.

On the other hand, Justin* acknowledges his urges. "I am doing what I can to not only stay 'virtuous,' but to try to not let these urges rule my life." He realizes that he could step over the line. "I sometimes question why I have never taken my obsession one step higher. I am not saying having sex with a child, but just to gain a child's trust and innocently brush against them, or be the fun uncle at the pool and let them dive off of your shoulders."

Robert* is of the same mind. "I'm the same way. It'll be almost impossible for you to get rid of your urges for good. But you can learn how to control them."

Nigel* shares his key to managing urges. "I don't want to ever harm a child, and that's because I love them. It's the desire to protect a child that keeps me from acting on my urges."

Magnus* recognizes urges and has a plan to deal with them. "I was at the pool. I had an urge to touch C inappropriately if she got there. I was afraid of touching her sexually. I also had strong urges to touch other young girls inappropriately. I urged my mom to take me home."

Andrew* says chemical castration has helped him deal with inappropriate urges. "I'm on Lupron® and … feel like I've been really lucky with the way this has worked out for me…. It started working after about a month. At that point I lost any sort of feelings and urges too."

Caleb* notes that his urges decreased with age. "My urges were never so strong I needed to go with chemical castration, but as I am getting older my sex drive is lessening. I really don't mind."

Nitro* points out that "some have to consciously battle urges. Others would say that they have attractions, but not urges."

Wade* observes, "For some people, resisting urges is easier than others. I don't think I would ever act on mine against children."

Potential Risk Factors

The Sexual Abuse Risk Assessment (SARA) identifies 25 potential risk factors (ASAP, 2015). Some members of the forum take exception to the inference that all pedophiles pose a risk to children.

Ethan* expressed his concern. "I fear that a

pedophile first coming to VP who feels bad about himself and hates his attraction could see this list as imposing some level of obligation. I don't think it does.

"Now, for pedophiles who are realistically nervous about possibly offending, then it makes sense to do whatever it takes to make sure you don't offend…. If someone does not feel they are a danger, especially if they have navigated opportunities and temptations in the past, I don't think they need to pay much attention to this list….

"In some cases, a single factor can completely resolve the problem. 'Do not spend time alone with a child you find attractive' could make the entire rest of the list irrelevant."

Afuche* also advised against discussing risk factors. "[It] is, in my opinion, buying into the false narrative that pedophile = criminal or sex fiend, and is contrary to the purpose of a book designed to help people understand pedophiles better."

There is no "one size fits all" in helping people with pedophilia. Something that may increase the risk for one person might not affect another or may actually decrease their risk. Some risk factors are static, while others can change over time, with or without intervention.

The SARA identifies risk factors which have been correlated with recidivism among sex offenders, but the validity and reliability of these factors have not yet been demonstrated for people with pedophilia who have never offended. I include a brief mention of some of the most significant factors so that those who feel at risk may focus on the ones that can be changed in order to manage any potential risk of offending.

Gender. Males are more likely to sexually abuse children than females and may find it crucial to take greater precautions to prevent abuse or false allegations. "Approximately one out of 20 men and approximately one out of 3,300 women are sexual abusers of children" (Abel & Harlow, 2001).

Age. The risk based on age is highest during puberty and decreases thereafter with age. "Advanced age is as likely to similarly diminish the frequency of sexual behavior involving children as it does other paraphilically motivated and normophilic sexual behavior" (APA, 2013, p. 699).

Intensity of Attraction. Those who are exclusive in their sexual attraction to children are often at greater risk than those who also have some attraction to adults. Exclusives may find it beneficial to develop non-sexual relationships with adults and should be allowed to make use of any outlet for their fantasies that does not cause harm to a child.

Current Relationship. An intimate relationship with another adult can lessen the risk of sexually interacting with a child. "Family level risk factors include difficulty establishing and/or maintaining appropriate intimate relationships and a chaotic, unstable, or violent home environment" (Tabachnick &

Klein, 2011, p. 16). More than half of those who completed a VirPed poll were not in a relationship with an adult or had never been in an adult relationship.

Satisfaction with Intimate Relationship. Those who are dissatisfied in their relationship with an adult may be at greater risk than those who are very satisfied with the status of their relationship, including those who are happily single. "Fathers who suspect the paternity of a child, are unattractive to potential female partners, and are dissatisfied with their current marital or common-law relationship would also be at greater risk" (Seto, 2008, p. 161).

Experience of Sexual Abuse. Those who have been abused *may* be more likely to abuse. "Childhood sexual abuse may be a risk factor for the onset of sexual offending, but it is not a necessary or sufficient factor" (Seto, 2008, p. 160).

Beliefs about Sex with Children. Engendering hope that one can live a happy life within the law is one of the most effective methods of risk reduction, since thinking abuse is inevitable makes it more likely to happen. Believing that adult-child sex does not harm children or that children can provide informed consent makes it more likely that the person will sexually interact with a child. "Dynamic risk factors are defined here as changeable (e.g., antisocial attitudes and beliefs about sex with children) or temporally fluctuating … factors that could, in principle, be targets of intervention" (Seto, 2008, p. 150).

Coming Out. While no one should be outed or forced to come out, having a caring person who knows that a person is sexually attracted to children (whether a relative, a friend or a therapist) can certainly help prevent them from sexually acting out with a child. Of those who completed a VirPed poll, 87% had come out to someone.

Employment. People with pedophilia are often able to work with children without abusing any of them, but it does increase the opportunity for abuse. Among VirPed members who work with children, there was no evidence that any member of the VirPed forum does so with the purpose of grooming the children for a sexual encounter.

Children in the Home. Some people with pedophilia choose to not have children, while others find that they are not sexually attracted to children they have raised from birth. The Westermarck effect alludes to the fact that "people who live in close domestic proximity during the first few years of life become desensitized to sexual attraction" (Wikipedia, 2015).

Time Spent with Groups of Children. Many people with pedophilia find that spending time with groups of children reduces the risk that they might abuse a child, while others choose to avoid being with children altogether. Of those who completed a VirPed poll, only 8% avoid being around children because they are afraid they might act on their urges.

Time Spent Alone with a Child. Spending time

alone with a child that a person is sexually attracted to increases the opportunity to sexually interact with that child. This is a risk factor that can generally be controlled.

Libido. SSRIs (Selective Serotonin Reuptake Inhibitors, often prescribed for depression) may reduce a person's libido and make sex drive more manageable. Individuals who have difficulty controlling their urges might choose chemical castration with testosterone blocking medications, although drugs can have negative side effects. Unlike physical castration, the effects are not permanent if the drugs are discontinued. Castration does not change a person's sexual orientation.

Undetected Abuse. If a person with pedophilia has had sexual contact with a child or viewed child pornography but the offense has not been detected by the authorities, some people will be more likely to do it again. On the other hand, the feeling of guilt may cause other offenders to be more determined not to abuse again.

Use of Inhibition-Reducing Drugs. "Dynamic risk factors are defined here as changeable ... or temporally fluctuating (e.g., level of alcohol intoxication) factors that could, in principle, be targets of intervention" (Seto, 2008, p. 150). Controlling the present and future use of drugs (including alcohol) is possible, but may require professional assistance.

Therapy. Some pedophiles find sufficient support through online forums. Others feel the need to talk to someone in person or want a therapist to help them deal with other issues in the context of their pedophilia. The German Prevention Project Dunkelfeld has proven to be successful in helping people with pedophilia who have not come to the attention of the criminal justice system (Beier et al., 2009). Of the 87 who completed a VirPed poll about therapists, 42% indicated that they found therapy helpful and another 15% thought they needed a therapist.

Afuche* writes, "I see risk as a continuum. Just about everybody is capable of hurting others, but that doesn't mean they're going to hurt anyone. Risk is comprised (like they say in detective shows) of means, motive, and opportunity. And there are varying levels of each according to the person and situation."

Tony* adds, "I have little faith in assessments, as they are often based on people released from prison, looking for certain circumstantial factors rather than on someone's support system, plan, views, beliefs, etc.... Risk is a rather abstract concept. For some, seeing themselves as a risk is a hindrance and gives the idea of a ticking time bomb, rather than a more realistic way of viewing themselves. For others, they might gloss over their triggering situations and not view what they can handle realistically."

There will never be a crystal ball that can determine which non-offending pedophiles will eventually abuse a child. If someone is sexually attracted to children and wants to make sure that they never molest anyone, it is important that they are honest with themselves. If they find themselves at risk of abusing a child, they should seek help ASAP.

CHILD SEXUAL ABUSE

Although pedophilia should never be conflated with child sexual abuse (CSA), there is an obvious relationship between the two. While the majority of people with pedophilia have never had sexual contact with a child (Dombert & Schmidt et al., 2016), a significant percentage of CSA is indeed perpetrated by pedophiles.

CSA was all too common in the world that I was born into in the 1950's. Four of my older sisters and a brother were sexually abused as children. My mother and her sister had been sexually abused by their father. My father and his brother had been molested by their mother. The problem was not just in my family either. Many of my friends suffered from CSA. I have witnessed the negative consequences of CSA over the past sixty years. Early on I determined that I would not abuse a child because I did not want to make anyone's life miserable.

What is CSA? According to Butcher et al. (2012),

> The prevalence of childhood sexual abuse depends on its definition, which has varied substantially across studies. For example, different studies use different definitions of "childhood," with the upper age limit ranging from 12 to as high as 19 years. Some studies have counted any kind of sexual interaction, even that which does not include physical contact (e.g., exhibitionism); others have counted only physical contact; others have counted only genital contact; and still others have counted consensual sexual contact with a minor. Depending on which definition is used, prevalence figures have ranged from less than 5 percent to more than 30 percent. However, even the lowest plausible figures justify concern. (p. 498).

One study found that "sixty-seven percent of children experience sexual abuse" (Crespi, 2009, p. 273), while more conservative estimates suggest that one in five girls and one in twenty boys is a victim of child sexual abuse (Finkelhor, 2012). Any amount of CSA is too much.

When does a child become an adult? The transition from childhood to adulthood is a process that can be different for each child, and while age of consent laws may be necessary, they are absolutely arbitrary.

Abe* observes, "I don't see the age of consent as *the* defining line between when an individual can or can't consent to sex. I believe the AoC is a preventive measure to assure that kids get to wait with sex for longer than it is in some cases necessary rather than it happening too soon with permanent and detrimental consequences."

Ethan* responds, "This inevitably happens when society tries to draw a line based on age. There are 10-year-olds who could vote intelligently, and all too many 50-year-olds who can't, but drawing a line at (say) 18 is an approximation that works."

What constitutes sexual abuse? An amicable relationship between two teenagers that lasts a lifetime is sometimes considered child sexual abuse. Urinating in public can be treated as a sexual offense and can cause the person to be included in the sex offender registry. But do such things really constitute sexual abuse?

The clinical meaning of CSA is not always the same as the legal definition, which may include statutory rape of older adolescent minors. Most professionals are particularly concerned when the child is prepubescent (generally under the age of 14) and the perpetrator is at least 16 years old and at least five years older than the child (APA, 2013).

Santrock (2009) depicts sexual abuse:

Sexual abuse includes fondling a child's genitals, intercourse, incest, rape, sodomy, exhibitionism, and commercial exploitation through prostitution or the production of pornographic material (p. 536).

An exact definition of child sexual abuse can be difficult to describe. Art* writes, "Being anti contact, for me, is being anti any contact they do not want or that could harm them."

But Ethan* points out that "adults are sometimes obliged to touch kids in ways they don't want (think hairwashes, medical exams, and grabbing them before they run into the street) and that's not sexual contact. Things such as beating a kid qualify as harmful contact but not sexual contact…. Whether a pedophile gets sexual enjoyment out of a hug isn't important; it's how it is perceived by others including the child."

Unwanted sexual advances toward an adult are considered abusive, but any sexual advances toward a child are considered abuse, whether or not the child enjoyed it.

Sexual abuse includes any act that is done for the purpose of sexual arousal of either party without the informed consent of both parties. Contact offenses involve sexual interaction with an actual child, even when there is no physical contact (voyeurism or exhibitionism). Distribution and viewing of images of children are referred to as non-contact offenses.

Motivation for Abuse

A variety of factors may cause a person to pursue sexual contact with a child. Older children are sometimes sexually curious about younger children. Professional assistance with family support *may* help a child outgrow this interest (Letourneau, 2017).

Less than one out of a thousand of those who molest children have no moral scruples about such boundary violations. Antisocial, psychotic perpetrators may be subject to civil commitment under sexually violent predator laws.

Individuals who are not generally attracted to children may choose children as surrogates because it is convenient to sexually interact with them rather than seeking out an adult partner. Situational offenders respond well to therapy.

The focus of this book is on those who might initiate sexual contact with a child because they have some level of sex drive that is directed toward children, which they did not choose and cannot change.

Researchers agree that girls are more often sexually abused than boys. Boys are less likely to report any sexual interaction with an adult, sometimes because they do not consider it abuse. Women also sexually abuse both boys and girls but much less frequently than do men. It is less likely to be reported because women are generally considered to be nurturers. In most cases, child molesters are men who have some type of sexual contact with young girls.

According to the child molestation prevention study (Abel & Harlow, 2001), the potential child molester might be a family member (50% are sexually abused by someone they live with), other relative (another 30% are sexually abused by someone they are related to but not living with), friend (10% are sexually abused by someone they know but are not related to), or stranger (only 10% are sexually abused by a stranger).

Survivor Stories

In a VirPed poll with 535 participants, 23% said there was sexual abuse in their childhood before the age of 14; 8% had childhood sexual experiences with an adult or another child at least four years older than themselves which they did not consider abuse; and 23% had sexual experiences with children in their age group which they did not consider abuse. Some children seem to be more traumatized by sexual contact than others.

Caution: the following stories may trigger negative feelings for some readers.

Indigo* describes what she experienced. "First let me say up front that sexual abuse of any child is wrong, hurtful, and should be punished. I was abused for years as a child by multiple different adults. I actually had a fairly happy childhood and the abuse didn't seem to negatively affect me. I remember to some extent even enjoying it. Please don't assume I am saying child molestation is harmless or healthy. It is a horrible scourge. It did a lot of damage to me, but at that time I couldn't see it.

"I read an article at 12 years of age about abuse, its affects and how it hurts children. This particular article detailed how abuse victims spiral into drugs, prostitution, broken relationships, and failed marriages. I read as much as I could on the subject for months. I can remember indirectly being told I was 'an empty shell,' that 'my innocence was gone—stolen from me,' that I was 'damaged, broken, and not worth as much as the other children.' I was convinced by society that no man would ever want me and that made me feel ashamed and disgusting. Of course these articles did not directly say that, but there were indirect statements that left me thinking this.…

"My abusers did a lot of damage, but society and its reactions easily did just as much damage. Even when I tell people that I'm OK they almost don't believe it, as if I should be a homeless prostitute. As an abuse victim I don't have to be broken or damaged.… I'm not an empty shell. Maybe it's OK to just be OK. Abuse doesn't have to ruin your life. It's a setback but it doesn't have to destroy you."

A Girl* agrees. "I had a sexual experience as a child that I do not consider to be abuse. I don't believe that what was done to me was *right*, but I refuse to feel abused, no matter how many therapists insist that I was. When I was five years old, a teenage boy started a sexual relationship with me. I did not reciprocate his interest in sex play, but I had a fascination for teenage boys and … he promised to take me places and to participate with me in the activities that I enjoyed.

"My friend did not ever hurt me. He did not attempt penetration…. I felt mildly guilty about what we did together, because I knew it was dirty and wrong…. I did not feel victimized, because I was not powerless in the 'relationship.' If I didn't want to do something, I told him no. If he continued to pressure me into activities I was not comfortable with, I made sure he wouldn't want to do it again….

"It ended when my friend didn't hold up his end of our bargain. He was only interested in spending time with me if we were hidden away doing naughty things. He didn't want to be my real friend, and he didn't want to take me with him when he did the cool, fun, teenage boy things that I wanted so much to be a part of. It was with reluctance that I finally gave up and told him our deal was off…. This boy remained in my life until I was eight years old, but we were no longer friends. I still played with his two younger brothers, but he barely even looked in my direction after that. I don't feel bad for myself…. I do worry that this boy may have moved on to abuse other girls who were more fragile."

Marie* describes her incest from the age of 7 to 14.

"The sex did not seem as bad to me as the fact that our father abandoned us."

Kay* points out, "I was not abused as much as my older sister, but the damage was just as severe and long-lasting. A child can be harmed even if you don't actually have sexual contact."

Jacob* writes, "When I was around 10, the 15 year old daughter of a family friend, stayed over one night. What started as a normal game of dares turned into her kissing and masturbating me. Later when I was 14, my mum went away for a night and asked her to come look after me. She brought a load of alcohol which I drank and we ended up having sex. After that she told me not to tell anyone and I didn't really see her again."

Ivan* writes, "I was sexually abused when I was 11 years old, by my babysitter, who was 18 at the time. I guess at first I didn't know what to do. At the end, he told me that whenever he comes over I should be ready for him and be naked on my bed…. I would shake when I would hear the door open. This continued to happen until I started to thin out nearing the age 13. He then stopped coming around, as I didn't need a babysitter."

Kyle* describes his abuse, "I was sexually abused as a young child. The man who was sexually abusing me was also physically and emotionally abusive. It caused me severe physical and emotional pain back then, and I'm still dealing with the emotional pain. I often still believe in the things he told me, such as nobody would like me if they knew how disgusting I am…. I wasn't attracted to the man who abused me, but I can't deny that there were times when I really did enjoy it (he wasn't always violent), something I'm very ashamed of."

Harmful Effects

The potential for harm is great whenever an adult has any sexual interaction with a child. There may be physical damage to the child's genitalia or other body parts, although in many cases this is not evident. The child may feel betrayed and lose their trust in adults, who should be there to protect them from harm. They may find it difficult to enjoy appropriate sexual relationships later in life or they might become promiscuous.

Afuche* adds, "There are also several more potential harmful effects of sexual abuse, including post-traumatic stress disorder, eating disorders, increased suicide risk, depression, a wide variety of fears and anxieties, psychotic break, lifelong difficulties with forming and/or keeping relationships, educational and employment problems, increased risk the victim will abuse others, guilt and shame by friends and family, being ostracized and rejected, and pregnancy or abortion as a result of the abuse."

Controversial scientific research has revealed a more nuanced understanding of the harm caused by CSA (Rind, Tromovitch, & Bauserman, 1998). The authors make it clear that they believe adult-child sex is still wrong, even though the harm may not be as pervasive as previously thought. In particular, they found that boys perceive and experience less harm than girls. The study was condemned by the Congress of the United States, but the results were confirmed in a subsequent study (Ulrich, Randolph, & Acheson, 2005).

We view CSA from different perspectives or domains. *Morally*, adult-child sex will always be wrong. In the *social* domain, there have been times when it was acceptable for an adult to sexually interact with a child, but that is not likely to happen again. From a *legal* perspective, age of consent laws have risen in fairly recent centuries and are not likely to be lowered again. In the *medical* realm, pedophilia has been separated from CSA and is only considered a disorder when the person is distressed by the attraction or acts on it.

Primary Prevention

There are a variety of approaches to the prevention of CSA. Tertiary prevention helps stop the abuse from being repeated. ASAP seeks to prevent it from happening in the first place, mainly by helping people with pedophilia find support so they will not molest a child. Recent educational materials highlight the importance of bystanders getting involved to prevent abuse (Tabachnick, 2009). While adults are primarily responsible for protecting children, we can also help children learn how to protect themselves.

Some educators have used the "good touch, bad touch" approach, but do we really want to teach children that sex is bad, especially when it can feel so good? Perhaps it would be helpful to add "secret touch." Parents have sometimes warned their children about "stranger danger," but most professionals have come to realize that the greatest danger is often right at home. Pro-contact pedophiles have argued that we should empower older adolescents with the ability to choose and then teach them how to say "No."

One acronym used to help children remember what they can do to help protect themselves from abuse is RESIST:

Run

Escape

Scream

Ignore

Stay away

Tell

SEX OFFENDER TREATMENT

by RecoveringSO*

[This chapter consists of a sex offender's response to the sex offender treatment program (SOTP) that he completed. Although I do not agree with every detail, some of what he learned might be helpful to those who have not offended.]

Here are some of the things I think they got right:

1. **Responsibility**. Therapy attempts to instill in us that we are completely responsible for our choices and whatever situation we permit ourselves to remain in.

2. **Empathy**. SOTP attempts to educate us on the effects of violating another human being and attempts

to guide us towards compassion for others.

3. **Planning Ahead**. The treatment program attempts to instill in us the necessity to have plans in effect that reduce our availability for offense and for getting out of emotionally tricky situations.

4. **Recognizing Our Own Limitations**. It instills in us that we, as former offenders, have limitations of that which we can effectively handle; to recognize where those limitations lie, and to not exceed them.

5. **Awareness of Intent**. SOTP attempts to instill in us an awareness of our intent behind our choices. Offenders, present and former, have a propensity to lie to ourselves in regards to why we are doing some of the things we are doing. An example: "I'm going to So-and-So's house for a beer; it has nothing to do with his daughter. No. Nothing at all!"

6. **Support System**. It encourages us to build pro-active support systems consisting of others around us and to use that support system in times of need.

7. **Immorality of Our Actions**. In short, SOTP attempts to instill in us the realization that what we did was wrong!

Here's a growing list of the things I believe they got wrong:

1. **Avoidance/Escape**. SOTP depends almost entirely on avoidance/escape and lists of rules and

guidelines to remain harm-free. But as I have learned through experience, there will always be that time when those lists of rules and guidelines will fail and we will find ourselves in compromising situations or situations of opportunity. When that arises, the only thing standing between that child and an offense is what is inside us. A child in the presence of a former offender, when that offender has not been prepared for that situation, is a child at risk.

2. **Misinformation**. The effectiveness of their program success is overstated…. Handing out misinformation is potentially dangerous since acting on bad information usually leads to bad outcomes.

3. **Nature of Pedophilia**. Pedophilia is often presented in SOTP as a "condition," "sickness" or "compulsive disorder." It is none of the above. It is a sexual orientation. It is intrinsic, unchangeable, and immutable. Compulsive disorders may attach themselves to pedophilia; but that doesn't make pedophilia a compulsive disorder.

4. **Fear**. We are taught to fear everything pertaining to children; and this is unhealthy. I have lived too many years locked up in my home because I was afraid to venture forth or go anywhere or do anything, because, "OMG, there might be kids there!"

5. **Shame**. We are taught to be ashamed—not of what we have done but of who we are. Maybe this is a

necessity for a time. It needs to be ingrained into offenders that we are responsible for our behavior and what situations we permit ourselves to be in; and if shaming gets the job done, so be it. But once a client gets that into their head, accepts responsibility and demonstrates enough change in their behavior and thinking, it's time to move past it.

6. **One Size Fits All**. The generalized program seeks to treat "all" offenders of various propensities, motivations and issues. This is erroneous as different types of offenders have different motivations, attractions and behaviors. A "one size fits all" approach simply can't be effective for all involved.

7. **Addiction Model**. It is based on an addiction model, but pedophilia is not an "addiction." It is a sexual orientation. I can't speak for other forms of sexual offending; perhaps the "addiction model" approach may be suitable for porn users; but addressing every different kind of sexual offense as we would address chronic drug use is just silly.

8. **Static**. The rigidity of the program of the unyielding rules and policies does not incorporate the inevitability that the former offender will change. But our ability to cope with certain situations will change over time; usually and hopefully for the better, but sometimes for the worse. Our strategies for remaining harm-free must be dynamic because we, as human beings, are dynamic.

9. **Non-Integration**. SOTP does not provide adequate means for offenders to reintegrate into society; and the closer our crimes or propensities are towards children, the more this statement is true. While SOTP proponents would hotly debate this, consider first that children are a part of society. They are entrenched in our society and contact with children within society is inevitable.

Consider some of the rules: (1) Can't go where children congregate — family events, restaurants, libraries, museums, parks and movie theaters. (2) No intimate relationships with those who have children. (3) One example given in the workbook for avoidance techniques includes "Pick times to shop and eat out when children are less likely to be there." Do we want a bunch of sex offenders running around lonely and angry in the middle of the night?

The majority of child sexual abuse occurs in the home and offenders are not prone to nabbing a stranger, making many of these techniques instruments of alienation instead of instruments of necessary avoidance. The "instant offense" ideology is (in most cases) a myth, with the exception of some former offenders who may have impulse control issues. We are separated from the vast majority of activities, establishments, potential friends, religious and holiday events; and this level of alienation is unnecessary and harmful.

10. **Overly Concerned with Fantasy**. The link

between fantasy and action is not as clearly understood as many would have us believe. SOTP seems very concerned about being the "thought police" and seeks to enforce a change in our fantasy life. For a pedophile, especially a fixated exclusive pedophile, this isn't going to happen; we can no more change that attraction and the fantasies behind them than we can change a gay person's attraction and the fantasies behind them.

For some, the line between fantasy and reality is a broad line and clearly understood. For others, it is not. It would be more productive to help the offender understand the distinction between fantasy and reality and broaden the line instead of trying to force and coerce away fantasies the administrators don't want their clients to have.

11. **Catch-22's**. There are too many situations where, with SOTP, there is simply no right answer and we will be wrong, no matter what we do. I was working in an environment where a granddaughter of a coworker was often present and the place was small enough, avoiding her was impossible. SOTP would have me flee this situation; then worry about me for not having a job because this "statistically increased my risk of re-offense." Backing offenders into no-win situations creates resentment and distrust towards the treatment providers; not to mention the personal effects of feelings of frustration and failure.

12. **Sexual Motivations**. SOTP emphasizes that

child molesting is purely and entirely sexually moti-vated; that the prime and only motivation of our offending behavior was sexual gratification. I hold this to be in error. While the sexual gratification component cannot be dismissed, I hold that for some or many of us, sexual gratification was not the only motivation and may not have even been the primary motivation.

13. **Stuffing the Model**. Our life has to fit the model of offending chosen by the administrator. I fail to see the value of stuffing our lives into a model, even if it doesn't really fit. It will not give us any real solutions to managing our behavior, as the techniques for managing that behavior are then devised from false pretenses.

14. **Fixation on the Cycle**. There is a death in the family. Well, how is this affecting your cycle? You lost your job. How is this affecting your cycle? Your medications are off. How is this affecting your cycle? Everything in our lives comes down to our offending cycle. This creates an atmosphere of fixation where, every little issue of our lives is centered exclusively around our propensity, real or imagined, to offend. Could this not, in itself, feed the fixation on offending fantasies and behaviors? Are you concerned about our cycle when we lose loved ones? Then grieve with us and help us resolve the grief; instead of reminding us that you think we're perverts. Not every issue in our lives is a threat to our harm-free life. Stop pretending

that they are.

RELAPSE PREVENTION PLAN

by Ian*

[In this chapter, Ian* has adapted the relapse prevention plan that he developed while at the Centre for Addiction and Mental Health in Toronto. While not all of these strategies are necessary for a non-offending pedophile, each person with pedophilia should develop a safety plan that works for them.]

This plan is a detailed list of strategies and techniques that I have learned and developed in order to avoid offending. The core of this plan includes:

1. Identification of High Risk Situations. Being able to identify risk is the key to successfully understanding and mitigating situations that could potentially lead to an offense. Although most non-offenders make a solemn commitment to not offend, underestimating the risk of daily situations can lead to failure. Risk is not an all or nothing proposition. Risk is a sliding scale. Those who say they are not at risk are just fooling themselves into letting their guard down.

For people with pedophilia, there are two categories of high-risk situations: environmental and emotional. Environmental situations occur when the person is either in places or with people that potentially could cause an offense. Emotional situations occur inside the person's head—how they are feeling and how cognizant they are of their emotional state.

I have identified the following environmental situations that would be high risk for me:
- Viewing legal pornography.
- Being at a public beach with children around.
- Being at or near a public school.
- Being on the internet with no safeguards.
- Participating in phone sex.
- Watching television alone at night.
- Being around other pedophiles.
- Being around groups of children.
- Being at a strip tease club/bar.

This is not an all-inclusive list, but they are key situations that could cause me to be at higher risk for wanting to offend. Using the coping strategies in this plan, I will be able to deal with these kinds of situations with the goal of not offending.

The following emotional situations are high risk: Feeling sexually frustrated, lonely, depressed, anxious, angry, aroused, deprived, hopeless or bored. I know these emotional states are potentially high risks for me, and I will utilize the coping strategies that I have learned to properly deal with my emotions and thoughts. Understanding what kind of environmental and emotional situations are high risk is key in allowing me to use my coping strategies in order to deal with these situations.

2. Identification of Cognitive Distortions. Almost all offenders use cognitive distortions in order to justify their behaviour/offense. Using these types of thinking errors makes it easier to offend. It is critical for me to be able to identify when I am having a cognitive distortion and to use my coping skills to deal with them.

Here are some cognitive distortions that I used when committing my offense:

- "I am not hurting anyone."
- "The girls in the pictures are not real."
- "I can't stop myself."
- "I am a victim."
- "Lots of other people do it."
- "I won't get caught."
- "I can stop anytime if I really want to."
- "It is just a sexual outlet."

Allowing these kinds of thoughts to go through my mind unchallenged can lead to offending. Additionally, there are more subtle cognitive distortions such as Seemingly Unimportant Decisions that can lead to offense. An example would be if I went to the lingerie website to buy my wife a birthday gift. Although it seems okay, I might see outfits on the site of women dressed in schoolgirl/little girl outfits, and that may lead me to offending. There is also the Abstinence Violation Effect, in which I may decide I've already lost control (by looking at adult women dressed as schoolgirls) and decide I might as well act out more by looking at younger girls online. I might decide that the positive aspects of offending (i.e., pleasure) outweigh the negative consequences.

3. Fantasy Management Strategies. Sexual fantasies and urges related to child pornography could consist of thoughts or visual images of an illegal sexual act (such as sexual activity with a person who is too young to consent) or illegal sexual images (such as pornographic images of children). Many groups have reported that they fantasized about child pornography before actually viewing it and/or that they fantasized about child pornography at times they were not viewing it. Some fantasies are very elaborate and drawn out, but even a brief thought or image is a fantasy. Fantasizing about sexual activity with children increases the risk for using child pornography. Masturbating to fantasies about children is an even bigger risk for use of child pornography.

Although many group members report having

sexual fantasies about children, or sexually arousing thoughts about child pornography, the most important thing to learn is how to manage these fantasies. It is not possible to make these fantasies go away forever, but it is possible to learn how to manage fantasies. The first step is to recognize when a thought or fantasy occurs, and when management strategies can be implemented to mitigate this situation. These strategies include:

• Mindfulness. Be aware of the thought, mental image, or fantasy and acknowledge that it exists, then let the thought float away without engaging it.

• Distraction. Do something until the fantasy passes by. Engage in an activity that will occupy the mind, such as reading, exercise, meditation, playing hockey or doing housework.

• Non-sexual fantasizing. Think about non-sexual activities that are pleasurable, such as climbing a mountain or building a shed. The more detailed the replacement fantasy, the more effective this strategy will be.

• Contact other people. Talk to someone else and let them know you are struggling. Tell them what management strategy you are using to deal with the issue. Telling another person takes away the secrecy and helps gain a sense of control over the fantasy.

• Thought stopping. When a fantasy is noticed (recognized), say "STOP!" to oneself. Imagine a stop sign. Think of it over and over and over again. This is an excellent way of jolting the mind out of a fantasy.

• Adverse imagery/consequence fantasy. Remind yourself of the negative consequences of engaging in inappropriate sexual fantasies and behaviour. Imagine yourself being arrested, going to court, being brought to prison. The more detailed and realistic the thoughts, the stronger the emotional response and the quicker the sexual fantasy will cease.

• Empathy for the victims. Think of what a child would go through in the production of child pornography. Think of how that child would feel and think while being forced to perform sexual acts. Think of how that child would feel after the act is committed. Think of how the act would affect the child in later years, and how it would influence their future relationships.

• Self-statements. Remind yourself that pedophilic fantasies and urges will pass; they are only temporary. Remind yourself of the consequences of committing a sexual offense upon you and your family and friends. "You are better than this." "You can deal with this." "I love my wife and family." "I love being free."

4. Emergency Coping Strategies. In addition to handling fantasy situations (which occur in my head), I can also wind up in high-risk situations in daily life. I want to be prepared for emergencies so I can successfully deal with them when they arise. I must be willing to accept that I will face emergency situations in the future, and plan in advance with how to deal with them. These emergency strategies can be used at anytime, but are especially useful when the risk is very high and I am in danger of acting on an urge to offend. In addition to the strategies already mentioned, I can leave the situation entirely. If the risk is too high, simply removing oneself from it is often the best way to deal with it.

5. Life Style Changes. Here are some life style changes that I am committing to:

• Participate in a prevention group. Participating in this group on a perpetual basis is essential to keeping me grounded and in touch with my efforts to not offend. It provides me a safe, supportive environment to express my thoughts and concerns.

• Improve my relationship with my wife, who has been my key supporter. She has been the pillar which I've built my life around. I need to continually ensure that we have excellent communication and that both our needs (emotionally, mentally, physically) are being met in a healthy, productive way.

• Ensure my children's safety. The single biggest change in my life is that I can move back home. Key to this change is ensuring that my children and I are kept safe at all times. That means I can only be in the house and around my kids while being supervised by an approved adult (currently my wife, my in-laws, and my parents). If an unsupervised situation presents itself, I must remove myself immediately. This is always possible!

• Think about the future. At some point my

children are going to grow up and be in relationships of their own. This plan is for the rest of my life, as I will likely have to deal with grandchildren and great-grandchildren. The rules I have now will apply well into the future, for the rest of my life!

• Daily physical activity. I use the acronym TYME to remind me of Tai chi, Yoga, Meditation and Exercise. My goal is to participate in one or more of these activities every single day, regardless of what is going on in my life (i.e., holidays, business trip, family emergency, etc.)

• Spend free time with others. Instead of being on a computer during my free time, I choose to spend it with my wife, family and friends. This is an excellent way to improve my mental health and personal growth.

• Be a good Buddhist. I have chosen to focus on the tenants of that religion—doing no harm, staying in the moment, and being mindful of my thoughts and feelings. This involves daily meditation and accepting the following five precepts every single day: refrain from killing, stealing, sexual misconduct, taking intoxicants and lying/gossip.

6. Computer Use and Internet Safety. Another big change in my life is that I am allowed to use computers, the internet and mass media storage devices. If I choose to use these tools in the future, I must ensure there are safeguards in place to give me time to identify and deal with high-risk situations. I do feel that using the internet is a risk for me, but I think it can be managed with help from my wife, as well as my social support structure. Here are some self-imposed restrictions that I place on myself:

• I will only be able to use one computer in the house in order to access the internet. This computer will be a desktop (not a laptop, mobile or tablet) and it will be set up in a "public" area of the house. The computer will not have a password on it, and the screen will always face away from the wall so anyone can see what is on the screen at any time.

• This computer will have parental controls installed that I will not be able to modify. These controls will restrict my access to the internet and prevent me from using the tools that I used during my offense; Internet Relay Chat, Peer-to-Peer Networking and BitTorrents.

• Even with limited internet access, this computer will have time restrictions on it. The internet will not work on this computer between the hours of 10 p.m. and 7 a.m. This was the time during which my offense occurred.

• I will have a "token" beside this computer at all times, "Buddhism: Plain and Simple" which is a book by Steve Hagen that I had while in prison. This token will not only remind me of the consequences of offending, it will serve as a reminder to mentally "check-in" before using the internet (i.e., How do I feel? Am I sexually frustrated, anxious or stressed?) All of these emotional states put me at greater risk.

• Any other devices that I have (i.e., phone, e-book reader) will not have internet access on them. I will only be able to access the internet via the one controlled computer.

• Although my wife will set up the restrictions and controls on my computer, ultimate responsibility for my compliance will not rest with her. I have a sponsor that is committed to helping me not offend and will report me to the police if I do offend.

• I must have a purpose. I cannot use the internet as a time waster. I will only use the internet if I have a reason to be on it (i.e., checking my e-mail, looking up something on Wikipedia, checking the weather). Mindlessly "surfing" puts me at a greater risk.

7. Social Support Structure. I have a great deal of support from my family and friends during my recovery. This is a list of people that I can talk to if I need support and advice. They are all aware of my situation and are all committed to helping me not offend. I keep a list of 10 people with their cell phone numbers. These people are aware of my offense, and are committed to assisting me in rebuilding my life and making healthy choices for the future. They are all available at any time to provide me support and advice when I need it. I have taken advantage of this on many occasions and will continue to do so for the rest of my life.

8. Reasons for Not Wanting to Offend. I have come up with five good reasons that I would not want to offend and get into trouble:

1. I do not want to hurt my wife, children, family, friends and/or employer in this way ever.

2. I do not want to victimize those children in the pornographic material.

3. I want to be mentally healthy which will lead to a happy, productive life.

4. I want to be free!

5. I do not want to betray society's trust, since I have been given a second chance!

9. Building Core Values. During the relapse prevention training, I was asked to target three key areas, which I will commit myself to work on. These areas were selected from the following: [1] Marriage/Couple/Intimate Relationships, [2] Parenting, [3] Family Relations, [4] Friends/Social Relations, [5] Career/Employment, [6] Education/Training/Personal Growth and Development, [7] Recreation/Leisure Activities, [8] Spirituality, [9] Citizenship, [10] Health/ Physical Well Being.

1. Marriage/Couple/Intimate Relationships. I know that I am very lucky to still be with my wife. I want to continue to build a strong, trusting relationship with her and I know there are still issues that I must deal with. With her assistance and support, I can rebuild my mental health and enjoy my life.

2. Spirituality. I want to put more time and effort into being a Buddhist. I know that the foundations of

this philosophy are in line with where I'd like my mind to be.

3. Health/Physical Well Being. I am committed to improving my physical health by employing TYME—doing Tai Chi, Yoga, Meditation and Exercise at least once per day, every day. This will be an excellent, healthy way to deal with anxiety and stress, and will be the substitute for less healthy options that I have turned to in the past.

Summary. Using this prevention plan is critical to my success as a participant in our society and as a strong, healthy member of the community. The most important things I must remember are:

• I am responsible for how I act.

• I can control and deal with thoughts in my mind.

• I have the skills to cope with situations as they arise.

• I am committed to staying with the changes I've made in my life.

• I have many people that I can get help from at any time.

• I do not want to offend and I have very good reasons for that.

This plan is a living document. It will change over the years to come, but the two constants are that this document will always exist and that I am committed to following the plan to live a long, happy life.

COPING STRATEGIES

People with pedophilia do not all experience irresistible urges to sexually assault children. Many have developed coping strategies to deal with the attraction without abusing a child. Coping mechanisms are also directed at dealing with the hatred and hysteria manifested by society against MAPs, even those who do not act on their attraction.

Trash* has internalized this hatred in his choice of a pseudonym. "I'm having a very hard time coping with the knowledge that we are hated. I see it everywhere— on reddit, on twitter, in discords, from friends, from family, on the news, in the paper.... Everywhere I look, every person I interact with, all I can see is the hatred of me. I can't win. If I keep my attraction a secret from everyone, I get to listen to anti-pedophilia hate and internalize it. If I'm open about my attraction, I get to feel that hate redirected straight to me."

Cat* responds, "The more I accept myself, the less their judgment matters to me. It takes time to accept yourself though."

Todd writes, "Eventually you just grow numb to it. I am mostly at that point, although occasionally a troll will still get to me. It just pisses me off, but then I will channel that adrenaline to productive ends and work out."

Like many pedophiles, Mara* has found a way to cope with the hysteria. "I don't read the comments sections on any topic, so I don't get upset and lose all faith in humanity. Usually people who have nothing better to do use the internet to vent their extreme views. Not worth it."

Silent* says, "I want to discuss the feelings I can best articulate as a sense of internalized discomfort or dysphoria over my orientation and the psychological effects of being minor-attracted in a hostile world. It seems to be that a self-critical tendency is inevitable for members of groups who are marginalized, and I'd like to reflect on how that's affecting me at the moment.

"While intellectually I can accept that this is what I am and I didn't choose what I'm attracted to, and that much of the mainstream discourse is misinformed at best, I can't entirely partition the social norms and signals away from my sense of self. So it's possible that an internalized MA [minor attraction] phobia is inescapable to some degree when we have no choice but to be what we are, and we are simultaneously forced to exist in a context that is alien and damaging. I can say that it's not me that is being so widely dehumanized and feared, but it still hurts when the end result is me second-guessing my motives and legitimacy as a person."

Tantric* adds another perspective, "I am a muggle in love with a non exclusive MAP. I do not hate pedophiles, I hate the act of child molestation and sexual abuse. I do not fault anyone with fantasies or thoughts or even being sexually aroused by minors. I do not wish harm on anyone, especially not someone afflicted with love for a demographic that cannot be consenting and therefore could morally never be a reality for them. I hope you can find some peace within yourself in knowing that not every person in the world believes that being attracted to children automatically deems you evil. You are not. This is a part of you yes, but there is so much more to you as well."

Some MAPs accept pedophilia as part of their identity (known as ego-syntonic), while others see it as intrusive from outside their real selves (ego-dystonic). In either case, it is important to accept the reality of its existence and the fact that it will probably continue throughout the lifetime.

Matt* introduced himself with "I didn't want to be here initially for fear that it would solidify the fact that I am in fact, a pedophile; but at some point one must embrace the reality and I am finally ready to do that."

Beachcomber* writes, "I must come to accept my sexuality and love and nurture it. We never act on it but we were created as sexual beings.... If I hate, despise and resent it, I'm hating a God-given part of myself, and these feelings only serve to eat me and destroy me from the inside out."

Nick* responds, "I don't think loving your sexuality is necessarily the goal. I don't love mine. If I could eliminate it, I would. Accepting it, and accepting yourself, is the key. I like myself. I think I'm a good person. I wish I wasn't sexually attracted to kids, but I don't beat myself up about it. I didn't choose this attraction, and I can't eliminate it, but I don't feel guilty about having it, and I won't, as long as I don't have sexual contact with a minor (and I won't)."

Masturbation

Some pedophiles use masturbation as a coping strategy to help deal with their attraction to children. Among both the professionals and people with pedophilia, there is a difference of opinion about whether masturbating to fantasies involving children is harmful or helpful.

The concept that fantasies will increase the likelihood of acting out in real life is based on the classical conditioning theory (Abel & Harlow, 2001). Max* posits that "using masturbation or sexual fantasies to help you to stop sexual urges in real life situations is like trying to kill fire by throwing oil into it!"

Adam* writes, "I've never had an orgasm and I'm too scared to start trying for one now; as I'm exclusive, the only way that would happen would be to think about children, and I don't want to link (what I believe to be) the positive feelings of orgasm with thoughts of prepubescents."

Kris* expresses concern about fantasies that involve children he knows. "Most of us will argue that fantasizing about young ones that we know is dangerous and can lead to misconceptions about behaviour based on our fantasies and desires and not based on objective real life interactions, and potentially doing something we shouldn't."

Stan* warns, "I would seriously recommend *not* fantasizing about kids you know. I used to do that frequently, and I feel it was one of the leading contributors to me offending."

Nick* separates his fantasies from reality. "In my opinion, sexual fantasies in and of themselves are harmless and I don't worry about them."

Personally, I seek to avoid masturbation altogether because of my conservative religious background, but I don't beat myself up, even when my fantasies involve children. We cannot control the thoughts that enter our minds, but we can choose whether or not we will entertain lust for another person.

I do not impose my values on those who maintain that fantasies actually relieve the sexual tension so they are less likely to act out with a real child. One research scientist "recommends that minor-attracted people be allowed to explore their sexuality through fantasy and pornographic material that does not involve actual children…. Contrary to popular belief, consuming child pornography does not cause a person to act out these fantasies in the real world" (Friedmond, 2013, p. 74).

Atlas* points out that "society has made being a pedophile a thought crime. People who are angry can outright scream things like 'I am going to kill you,' when they are feeling angry. Society understands them and understands that they were just talking and no one labels them dangerous. A lot of people fantasize, share, or even roleplay out 'rape fantasies' between adults and society does not consider them a danger either. Or think of all the video games in which people kill each other; with guns or otherwise." Some psychologists suggest that punching a pillow relieves the tension so you will not punch a real person.

Daywalker* believes that for him fantasies are a helpful outlet. "I find that the longer I go without masturbation, the hornier I get, not the other way around. When I go for longer than usual for whatever reason, not only do I find it harder to keep sexual thoughts about children from my mind, but I also seem to start noticing children who might normally be a little under my AOA in a sexual light."

Magnus* even thinks that fantasies about children he knows are beneficial. "I don't see anything wrong with it. It actually helps me resist temptation. It cuts down on feelings of lust towards the child in question."

Avoidance

Some pedophiles cope with their unwanted attraction by avoiding children altogether. They avoid getting married (or at least having children) and choose to work where there are no children. They may even choose to go shopping or spend time out in public only at times when children are not likely to be present. ASAP does not recommend this approach for everyone, but supports those who feel it is necessary or at least helpful.

Kumo* was told that he should avoid anything to do with children. "I really like shota and loli images (CL here) but my friend says that they're bad for me and I need to stop it, and stop playing as child-like characters in video games, or avoid any media with children in it."

Petri* observes that "you can't avoid children or images of children forever, yet it can be healthy not to be obsessed with them."

Tantri* adds, "Focusing on adult relationships since you're non-exclusive seems like a great idea. You do not need to avoid all things children to do this though as those feelings will need an outlet somewhere along the line."

Castration

Cat* describes his experience with castration, which is undoubtedly the most dramatic coping mechanism. "I did chemical castration through a strong dose of progesterone for about a year. I finally opted for castration instead. If you're looking for a cure, I'd say this is the best you can get, but it's a serious life choice that isn't to be taken lightly.

"I've been castrated for over 3 and a half years and I've been teaching at elementary school for almost 3 and a half years. I teach my AOA, kids aged 9-11. This year, I've even have the pleasure of teaching them health and sex ed! How ironic. The very weak sexuality lowers my urges to the point where I never worry about doing something I'll regret. I do still masturbate and have sex with my wife and I do still sometimes fantasize about children aged 11-12, but it doesn't bother me anymore."

Virtuous pedophiles have developed a variety of different coping mechanisms to deal with their attraction to children. Brian* says the "most helpful exercise was to make a list of all the people I would hurt." ASAP suggests that you use whatever strategies work for you.

PARADIGM PERSPECTIVES

There are a variety of approaches that are currently in use for the treatment of people with pedophilia who have not committed a sexual offense. An adaptation of the typical sex offender treatment program is most common, as discussed in previous chapters. Since very little scientific research has been done with non-offenders, this author does not recommend one method above the others and has talked with individuals who feel they have benefited from each of these paradigms. ASAP does not control the therapists to whom we refer clients or mandate that they use a certain approach. In the next chapter, we will consider some of the specific techniques that are used.

Note: A therapeutic relationship between the MAP and the treatment provider appears to be more significant for success than the particular model that is used.

Adaptation of Sex Offender Treatment Program

Convicted sex offenders are often *required* to complete a sex offender treatment program as a condition of probation, even though this conflicts with professional codes of ethics. "Clients have the freedom to choose whether to enter into or remain in a counseling relationship" (American Counseling Association, ACA, 2005, p. 4). Treatment professionals sometimes justify this use of force, claiming that clients can stay in jail and never see their families if they don't choose treatment. Non-offenders might be pressured into counseling by family or friends, but they are not mandated to submit to counseling.

The treatment program and assessment tools are based on an index offense, which of course is irrelevant to those who have not offended. Relapse prevention plans center around previous offending behavior. Some of the cognitive behavioral therapy might be helpful to non-offenders, but much of the therapy revolves around the abuse cycle that just does not fit.

While the offense model might be the only program available for non-offending pedophiles in some areas, be aware that much of it could be a futile attempt to change your views and your arousal patterns. I was trained in this approach by Gene Abel and know of at least one Virtuous Pedophile who felt he was helped by the Behavioral Medicine Institute of Atlanta, which uses this model.

Addiction Model

"Alcoholics Anonymous (AA) is an international mutual aid fellowship founded in 1935 by Bill Wilson and Dr. Bob Smith in Akron, Ohio" (Wikipedia, 2017a). AA has been adapted to deal with other addictions, including Sexaholics Anonymous (SA) and Sex Addicts Anonymous (SAA), which some non-offending pedophiles find helpful. Other treatment programs, often spawned by Dr. Patrick Carnes, deal with sexual addiction without the religious overtones.

While pedophilia is not an addiction or an obsession in itself, a person with pedophilia might become addicted to viewing pictures of children or become obsessed with sexual thoughts involving children. The recent emphasis on moderation rather than abstinence in dealing with addictions would not apply since the abuse of even one child is too much. I have received positive feedback from Virtuous Pedophiles who participated in The Prevention Project™ at Namasté (2017) Center for Healing, which uses an addiction model as part of a program that treats MAP clients and/or those who have a sex/porn addiction that has escalated into the compulsive viewing of child pornography and/or distressing fantasies about children.

Good Lives Model

"The Good Lives Model (GLM) is a strengths-based rehabilitation theory that augments the risk, need, and responsivity principles of effective correctional intervention through its focus on assisting clients to develop and implement meaningful life plans that are incompatible with future offending" (Prescott, undated.)

RESPONSE TO FEEDBACK

Both ASAP and VirPed have received positive support from mental health professionals and the public at large, but there have also been some valid concerns, which we will address in this chapter.

One of the most common responses we get is "We need to protect children, not help pedophiles." We are certainly interested in protecting children, but is it not possible to do both? Primary prevention includes providing mental health support to people with pedophilia so they will not molest children.

It is important to examine what we are doing to determine whether or not it really helps prevent CSA. Substantiated cases have indeed dropped 58% between 1992 and 2008, but there is evidence that the number of actual cases continues to increase. Tabachnick & Klein (2011) report:

A decrease in reported and substantiated cases may be different than a decrease in the incidence of child sexual abuse. They [Finkelhor et al.] offer six different hypotheses for this decline, one being that the public and professionals have become more reluctant to report child sexual abuse due to negative publicity (p. 14).

Public hysteria surrounding pedophilia tends to drive legislators to make tougher laws, but these do not necessarily prevent CSA and often make it less likely that abuse will be reported. For example, the sex offender registry can give a false sense of security from "stranger danger." The reality is that most offenders are not strangers nor are they on the list of offenders.

The types of cases that have typically given rise to more stringent SORN [Sex Offender Registration & Notification] policies – stereotypical stranger abductions of children – are statistically improbable events that occur approximately 115 times per year (Akerman, Harris, Levenson, & Zgoba, 2011, p. 150).

The registry would be more effective if there were tier levels, listing the nature of the crime, with the possibility of being removed from the list.

Even among those found on public registries, a distribution of risk exists, with a minority designated in most states as high risk, predator, or sexually violent (Akerman, et al., 2011, p. 157).

Another example of misguided legislation is mandatory reporting laws, which can inhibit people with pedophilia from seeking therapy (Zuckerman, 2008). Some people have expressed concern that I am not a mandatory reporter, but confidentiality is vital to a therapeutic relationship. According to one textbook, when individuals receive counseling that will help them become better citizens, the benefits to society outweigh the consequences of their refusal of counseling if confidentiality is not guaranteed (Remley & Herlihy, 2010). If disclosures made to a mental health professional by an individual who is receiving therapy were held in strict confidentiality, people with pedophilia would be more likely to receive support that could prevent them from sexually abusing children.

Some people think all pedophile groups are trying to lower the age of consent. Ethan* points out that it would be better for pedophiles to leave decisions about the age of consent to muggles, since we obviously have a vested interest. Age of consent laws are arbitrary and have varied significantly over time and from place to place.

Anton* observes, "We don't need lower age of consent laws. We only need to be recognized as people, instead of blood thirsty monsters and predators."

In response to Ender's* "Medium" article, "Yes,

'Our Kind' Will Be Accepted," David wrote, "It should not be treated as a group that should be somehow accepted."

Ender* replied, "Pedophilia (or any other unchosen condition) doesn't need anyone's 'acceptance' to exist. You can say you won't accept it as much as you want and it will continue to exist."

But David is understandably concerned that anyone would identify as a pedophile. "Call yourself a Christian not a virtuous pedophile."

I would not choose the word pedophile but pedophilia is the technical term used by professionals for individuals who are sexually attracted to children. My identity is rooted firmly in Christ, but I also have many other identities such as white, heterosexual, American, teliophile, etc. In the context of a discussion on sexuality, one does not say, "I'm Jewish."

Many muggles assume that all MAP groups are trying to legalize sex with children. David opines, "'Virtuous Pedophile' is an agenda term loaded with ulterior motives. It suggests degrees of perversion and lends credibility to discuss acceptable pedophile actions with children."

Ender* points out the difference between the non-contact stance of VirPed and pro-contact groups such as NAMbLA.

Although sexual interaction between adults and children may not always be harmful, any risk of harm to a child needs to be taken seriously. Finkelhor and Berliner's (1995) study indicated that "about 40% of children experiencing child sexual abuse have few or no symptoms on standard measurements" (Hunter, 2006, p. 351). While many scientists view these children as survivors rather than victims, they still believe that adult-child sex is wrong.

People often claim that children would never lie about being abused. Any child who discloses abuse should be taken seriously, but is it possible that they may have been pressured into developing false memories? Butcher et al. (2012) describe the repressed memory movement.

> Reports of a link between early sexual abuse and various forms of psychopathology began to emerge in the 1980s. After these reports came out, many therapists proceeded to suggest to their patients with such conditions that perhaps they too had been abused. For certain overzealous therapists, the fact that many patients had no memories of any abuse was taken as evidence that the painful memories had simply been "repressed." In other cases, a patient's simply having such common problems as difficulty sleeping or being easily startled was taken as evidence of past abuse. Over time, many patients became as convinced as their therapists that they must have been abused and that this accounted for their current difficulties (p. 25).

Some people emphasize punishment rather than prevention, even though there is no evidence that fear of punishment prevents abuse. While incarceration may delay further abuse, prison does not change the sexual orientation of a person with pedophilia.

Even some professionals assume that nothing can be done to prevent CSA from happening in the first place. There is a growing body of evidence that many current reactive practices are not effective in primary prevention since nothing is done until after a child is victimized. Primary prevention is a matter of public health and includes educating young people about healthy sexuality, developing protective policies for institutions that deal with young people, and providing therapy to people with pedophilia before they act on their attraction to children.

Some people assume that voluntary treatment will never work. The PPD provides empirical evidence that non-adjudicated pedophiles will come for treatment if they are guaranteed confidentiality in connection with an effective treatment program. From a German population of 80 million, 1740 people who acknowledged that they were sexually attracted to children voluntarily applied for the Dunkelfeld program in the first seven years of the program. (Beier et al., 2009).

Butcher et al. (2012) provide further assurance that there is hope:

> As our understanding of abnormal psychology expands, we are increasingly able to help patients

previously considered to be hopeless cases (p. 30).

An inappropriate sexual attraction to a deviant stimulus (such as prepubertal children) can be altered by pairing pictures of the deviant stimuli with a foul odor or another unpleasant stimulus (p. 90).

Therapy does not "cure" pedophilia or change the sexual orientation of a person with pedophilia, but it can reduce sexual arousal to children so that the desire does not lead to the deed. Assessment "outcome information can also be used in the counseling process. Some clients finding [sic] it very empowering to view assessment results that indicate they have made positive changes" (Whiston, 2009, p. 10).

VirPed founders address another frequently asked question, "Won't pedophiles talking to each other just embolden them to abuse children?"

According to the best available evidence, a pedophile is most likely to abuse a child when he or she feels desperate, isolated from the community, and feels there is nothing to lose. A forum provides a community to reduce isolation and desperation. The Virtuous Pedophiles forum provides a place where pedophiles can discuss living with their attraction, but with the shared understanding that sexual activity with children is wrong and that we are not trying to make it more acceptable. Many leading experts share our belief that participation should reduce the risk of child sex abuse.

Discussion of anything with erotic content is not allowed, nor is linking to any such material. We will not permit discussion, whatever the topic, that seems to be influencing any individual in the direction of offending.

Child sexual abuse thrives in secrecy. There is no evidence that anyone ever became a pedophile or a child molester because someone talked about it (Abel & Harlow, 2001).

Unloveable* writes, "It's a bit of sick irony that society's response to the problem of child sexual abuse is to alienate the pedophiles. This is probably the worst response imaginable if your interest is in reducing the overall amount of child sexual abuse in the world."

HOPE FOR THE FUTURE

Pro-contact MAPs would like to lower the age of consent, but sexual interaction between an adult and a child should never and will never become acceptable or legal. I do hope that the stigma surrounding pedophilia will diminish enough so that those who are sexually attracted to children will be able to seek mental health support without being treated like monsters who are destined to offend. Professionals must learn how to respond to minor attracted people in a way that will support non-offending behavior without attempting to change the person's sexual orientation. The primary goal of ASAP is to help non-offending pedophiles connect with supportive mental health professionals.

The VirPed (2017) founders address the question of what they want:

> We want society to recognize that we are not monsters lurking behind bushes waiting to pounce

on unsuspecting children, that many of us are good people who have a sexual attraction that we did not choose and cannot change, but are capable of controlling. Not only are pedophiles capable of being good people, many of us **are** good people.

A related question on the VirPed (2017) site is: "How could society change to make things better?"

If a pedophile wants help, society should make sure they can get it — before they harm a child. In Germany the Dunkelfeld project is open to those who have not broken the law, and in the United Kingdom there is a program known as StopSO. Globally, the Association for the Treatment of Sexual Abusers (ATSA) has become more welcoming of non-offending pedophiles. Our hope is that programs of this kind will become more prevalent.

Nick* shares his hopes for the future of the VirPed forum. "There is no master plan. The intent is just doing what we're doing—doing what we can to reduce stigma and doing our best to help each other lead happy, productive and law-abiding lives."

Ender* expresses his hope. "I know it's easy to succumb to the thought that everyone hates us and they all want to see us locked up, castrated or dead. However, I am more and more convinced that the rabid foaming-at-the-mouth haters are a (very vocal, I admit) minority and that we're facing increased awareness and understanding of what it means to be a pedophile and increasing social support for the plight of non-offending pedophiles. In the resources channel at the MAP Support Chat I've been collecting articles showing the media coverage of the phenomenon of non-offending pedophilia and the coverage has been growing exponentially since the first articles daring to suggest the existence of non-offending pedophiles."

Some of the specific hopes for the future that have been expressed by various Virtuous Pedophiles include:
- Availability of child-like sex dolls.
- Legalize virtual (drawn) child pornography.
- Change mandatory reporting laws.
- Real life groups for people with pedophilia.
- Being able to come out without repercussions.
- Get married and have children.
- Do away with civil commitment.
- Never punish thought crime.
- Just existing.

Ender* believes that "a significant majority of society *will* understand the difference between pedophile and child molester and *will* understand that it's unfair to vilify, demonize, ostracize and wish ill on people for an unchosen condition, and will realize that changing their attitudes towards us will lead to a much healthier society and a reduction in child sexual abuse."

Dan* shared his vision for the future, "As we conceptualize the erotic template of those with pedophilia, and try to de-stigmatize attraction to children, a simple and effective method is simply to not refer to those with pedophilia as pedophiles. This is a mainstream idea in mental health: a person is more than their disease. With pedophilia it seems the negative stigma is magnified so much more by saying 'he is a pedophile' versus 'he is a man with pedophilia.' Saying someone has pedophilia eliminates the conflation—they may or may not be a convicted child molester."

GLOSSARY

Abuse. Herein refers to the potential to cause harm, even if no harm is perceived.

Anime or **manga**. A particular Japanese style of comics not based on real children. Loli/lolicon is erotic stories with drawings of little girls. Shota/shotacon is of boys.

Anti-contact. Herein refers to those who oppose any type of sexual contact between an adult and a child. Not opposed to appropriate social contact with children.

AoA. Age of attraction. Approximate ages of those one finds attractive.

AoC. Age of consent. Arbitrary age at which one can legally consent to sex in a particular jurisdiction.

ASAP. Association for Sexual Abuse Prevention. A

non-profit organization founded in the state of Oregon in 2015 by Tabitha Abel, Todd Cooper and Gary Gibson to help connect minor attracted people with mental health professionals.

BEDIT. <u>Be</u>rlin <u>Di</u>ssexuality <u>T</u>herapy manual developed by Prevention Project Dunkelfeld.

BL. Boy lover. Person who is attracted to boys.

Child. Herein refers to a prepubescent individual under the age of 14.

CSA. Child sexual abuse. Anything done for the purpose of sexual arousal to a prepubescent individual under the age of 14 against their will or by an adult or person at least 5 years older.

DSM-5. *Diagnostic and Statistical Manual of Mental Disorders, Fifth edition*. List of mental conditions that are currently considered abnormal.

Ego-Dystonic. "Thoughts, impulses, and behaviors that are felt to be repugnant, distressing, unacceptable or inconsistent with one's self-concept" (Wikipedia, 2017b).

Ego-Syntonic. "Instincts or ideas that are acceptable to the self; that are compatible with one's values and ways of thinking" (Wikipedia, 2017b).

Ephebephile. An adult who is sexually attracted to mid- to late-adolescent minors (typically ages 15-17).

Exclusive. An adult who is sexually attracted only to prepubescent children.

GL. Girl lover. Person who is attracted to girls.

Hebephile. An adult who is sexually attracted to pubescent early-adolescent children (typically ages 11-14).

MHP. Mental health professional, including counselor, psychologist, psychiatrist or social worker.

MI. Motivational interviewing. A type of therapy that includes expressing empathy, rolling with resistance, developing discrepancy, supporting self-efficacy, and avoiding argumentation.

Muggle. Herein it is a term used for a non pedophile.

Offense. Herein it refers to a crime involving child sexual abuse.

Pedophile. An adult who is sexually attracted to pre-pubescent children (generally under the age of 14), whether or not they have acted on it.

Pedophilia. A sexual orientation, an enduring sexual interest in prepubescent children.

Pedophilic Disorder. The person has acted on the attraction to children or experiences marked distress or inter-personal difficulty because of it. The person is over the age of 16 and the object of their attraction is more than five years younger (APA, 2013).

PPD. Prevention Project Dunkelfeld. Premier therapy program in Germany for people with pedophilia who have not come to the attention of the criminal justice system.

Pro-contact. Being in favor of lowering the age of consent to make sexual contact with children legal.

PWP. Person with pedophilia. Emphasizes the person rather than the condition.

SARA. Sexual abuse risk assessment. Tool being developed by ASAP to identify risk factors that may cause a person with pedophilia who has not molested a child to be at risk of offending.

Sexual. Any action that has the intent of stimulating arousal.

Sexual Orientation. Direction of one's attraction on a gender axis and a developmental age axis.

Teleiophile. A person who is primarily attracted to mature adults.

Virtuous Pedophile. A person who is sexually attracted to children but is committed to never molest a child. When capitalized herein, it refers to a member of the VirPed peer support group.

APPENDIX 1:
PSYCHOTHERAPY FOR MAPs

[Reproduced in full with permission (B4U-ACT, 2017). Copyright B4U-ACT 2017. Note: The author of this book was part of the committee that developed this document.]

Minor-Attracted Persons, or MAPs, frequently hesitate to seek psychotherapy for fear of rejection, stigma, harmful treatment techniques or inappropriate reporting. Therapists may be uncomfortable or lack information about this population. This brochure has been developed collaboratively by therapists, MAPs and allies through the organization B4U-ACT to provide you with principles of ethical and effective treatment as well as further resources. There are very few studies on non-offending MAPs or therapy for them; therefore, this document cannot be considered definitive. However, it is based on our experiences providing and receiving psychotherapy, as well as on research on populations facing similar mental health issues, and emerging research on the needs of MAPs. B4U-ACT also promotes research into this population.

Who are MAPs?

- MAPs or Minor-Attracted Persons are people who are both emotionally and sexually attracted to children or underage adolescents.

- The term Minor-Attracted Person is preferred to the word "pedophile," which is often incorrectly understood to denote a person who sexually abuses children.

- A MAP may or may not have ever approached a child sexually.

What do we know about MAPs?

- Minor-attracted people do not choose to be attracted to children, but they can choose not to act on the attraction.

- Stigma, shame and fear keep many MAPs silent about their struggle.

- Many, perhaps most, MAPs have not offended

and will not harm those toward whom they feel affection. Conversely, many, perhaps most, who have offended are not MAPs; sexual offenses against children are often opportunistic or otherwise motivated. Studies of MAPs outside the criminal justice system show that many never offend.

• Both MAPs who have offended against a child and those who never have may seek support to live good lives within the law and their own consciences.

• MAPs may have other life challenges and psychiatric issues (e.g., depression, anxiety, interpersonal issues, loss, addictions, stage-of-life transitions) for which they want therapy, apart from their attraction to children or in tandem with it. However, MAPs may avoid therapy, fearing that the therapist will focus only upon that aspect of their whole being and on risk management.

What principles guide effective treatment?

• Trust. A relationship of trust is the most important aspect of any treatment program. Confidentiality is crucial, and therapists should be versed in the mandated reporting laws of their own states to avoid inappropriate or unnecessary reporting.

• Autonomy. Participation in therapy should always be voluntary. Clients should not be forced to participate in any particular therapeutic technique or program. Therapists should not serve as an extension of the criminal justice system; their primary responsibility is to their clients.

- Client-Centered Focus. Therapy for MAPs may focus on their minor attraction or not. Like others, MAPs are whole people with a variety of concerns and must be encountered as such, not stereotyped, demonized, or disregarded by changing the focus to prevention. MAPs, like any other client, know what support and assistance they need and should participate in deciding the focus of their therapy.

- Knowledge Base. The chief treatment error made by therapists is the conscious or unconscious belief that a MAP seeking treatment inevitably has or will molest a child. MAP-informed therapists understand that, while similarities to sexual offenders against children exist, significant differences between the two groups also exist, particularly in their management of their sexual feelings. These therapists understand the similarities and differences and treat their clients with evidence-based methods appropriate to the individual client. The preferred model of treatment is LGBT affirmative psychotherapy, which treats sexual feelings as innate, unchangeable and subject to personal acceptance. The American Psychological Association (APA, 2017) provides guidelines on its website (see below). Applied to the minor-attracted person, affirmative therapy separates sexual orientation from its expression, emphasizing acceptance and personal growth. This in no way endorses sexual contact between adults and minors. Awareness of the shame, stigma and fear of exposure that MAPs experience due to their sexual and emotional feelings is crucial to treatment. Therapists should provide a proper diagnosis but use caution in recording a diagnosis of Pedophilic Disorder, because the associated stigma can negatively affect treatment. All therapists can and should learn to treat MAPs. If they are unable to meet the needs of a client, they should make an appropriate referral. More research with non-forensic MAPs is required to develop evidence-based practice with MAPs. As with other disenfranchised communities, the principle "nothing about us without us" applies; treatment programs should not be developed without MAPs participating in the process.

What are the legal and ethical concerns?

- The approach advocated here is consonant with the ethical guidelines of the American Psychological Association, National Association of Social Workers, American Psychiatric Association and other professional organizations for psychotherapists.

- Regulations governing reporting of child abuse differ greatly from state to state. Lawful, effective, ethical treatment of MAPs requires knowledge of local reporting laws. Inappropriate or unnecessary reporting destroys the therapeutic alliance, while early transparency about reporting enhances trust – which can protect children.

• Supporting MAPs in living productive, ful-filling, respected roles within their community will promote their emotional stability and thereby help to keep the community safe.

What other resources are available?

• http://www.apa.org/pi/lgbt/resources/guidelines.aspx – American Psychological Association guidelines for affirmative psychotherapy.

• http://www.thisamericanlife.org/radio-archives/episode/522/transcript – This American Life podcast tells the story of a teenaged MAP seeking treatment.

• http://www.b4uact.org/ – advocates for ethical and compassionate mental health services for MAPs.

• http://www.asapinternational.org/index.html – brings together mental health professionals and individuals who are sexually attracted to children.

• http://virped.org/ – Virtuous Pedophiles, support and resources for MAPs who wish to live within the law.

APPENDIX 2:
TREATMENT TECHNIQUES

Some treatment techniques used by mental health professionals are specific for dealing with pedophilia, while others are of general use with a particular application for people with pedophilia. The following list is not intended to be exhaustive. Some of the techniques are not recommended for non-offending pedophiles, but they are described here so that readers can be familiar with the methods and terms that some therapists use.

Develop a Therapeutic Relationship

Acceptance. A therapeutic relationship is the key to any treatment, so it is vital to manifest unconditional positive regard for the person with pedophilia.

Recognize that attraction to children is not the same as acting on it. Do not treat the client like a monster or a ticking time bomb. Be willing to work with the client's view of pedophilia—whether as a sexual orientation, mental disorder, addiction or obsession. Acknowledge that you think it is never appropriate to sexually interact with a child, but do not enforce your values on the client. Help the client accept their condition and recognize that the attraction is not likely to change, but assure him/her that acting on the attraction is not inevitable. Avoid anything that might increase feelings of guilt or shame.

Rapport. Develop and maintain a trustworthy, therapeutic relationship with the client so you are working together toward a solution. Enhance comfort, trust, and safety. "What is it like for you to come to therapy?" "How was this first session for you?" Explain the counseling process without mystery or surprises.

Respect. Unconditional positive regard and acceptance. Treat clients with dignity so that they will become worthy of it. Recognize that therapy is an invasion of the client's privacy. Honor client's right to self-determination.

Active Listening

Rather than just giving advice, listen to what the client says and reflect what you heard. Respond to body language and facial expression, and communicate acceptance of the person with voice tone, as well as body language.

Brief verbals. Communicate "I'm listening" with "mm-hmm," "hmm," "gotcha," "okay," "right," "I get it," "I see," "go on," or selectively repeating one of client's key words.

Nonverbal attending. Observe client's behavior. Use eye contact, facial expressions, nods, body language, posture, and gestures to demonstrate active listening.

Paraphrase. *Reflection* that restates in your own words what the client said. If you get it wrong, the client can correct you.

Prompting. Similar to *furthering* to encourage the client to advance the story, but consists of *brief verbals* or nonverbal cues. "Go on." "And...?" Nod, curious expression, gesture, etc.

Reflection. *Paraphrase* or restate what the client said in your own words. Include feelings. Make it tentative. Demonstrates attentiveness. Solicit corrections.

Keep the Session on Track

Informed consent. Inform client of local mandatory reporting laws and under what circumstances you would feel it necessary to report. Begin with initial interview and continue throughout. Discuss the benefits and risks of therapy. Present therapy for non-offending pedophiles as developing and discuss the success of Prevention Project Dunkelfeld. Clarify client's role and your role.

Assessment. Most non-offending pedophiles who seek treatment will self-identify and share their gender and age of attraction. Actuarial Risk Assessment Instruments (such as the Abel® and the Stable®) are not designed for non-offending pedophiles, since they are based on an index offense. The SARA might be a useful tool to help the client evaluate any risk of offending. Appraise appropriateness of behaviors but do not assume that the client has offended or will inevitably offend. Evaluate fitness for group therapy.

Checking In. Informal assessment of the counseling process to make sure the counselor and client are on the same page and headed in the same direction.

Challenging. Mild *confrontation*. Specific and concise. Disagreement with client's misinformation or misconceptions. Identify client's contradictions or inconsistencies (facts, timelines, etc.). Tactfully request *clarification*. Phrase as "I don't understand...."

Clarification. Requesting more specific details or *challenging* client's conflicting information. Unfamiliar language, vagueness, unclear storyline, etc.

Confrontation. More robust *challenge* to client's assertions. Avoid accusations. Can be therapeutic if specific, focused, and tentative. Challenge behavior, without labeling the person. Identify discrepancies or implausibility. Encourage response and reconciliation.

Countertransference. Guard against superimposing something from your own experience onto the client, especially if you are a survivor of CSA. Strong feelings (positive or negative) toward the client must be managed. Seek supervision/consultation.

Diagnosis. Consider the benefits and downside of a formal diagnosis of pedophilic disorder. DSM-5 lists three criteria for a diagnosis, which also requires acting on the attraction or being distressed by it. The client may appreciate knowing that it is a treatable disorder but not want the term included in his or her medical records.

Directing. Keep sessions on track while respecting client's autonomy.

Focusing. Summarize multiple issues raised. Hone in on the most significant topic, limiting and prioritizing the number of issues to be processed at a given time. "Which would you like to concentrate on first?"

Furthering. Request additional details to encourage the client to continue the story to a deeper level. Preferably using *open-ended questions*.

Generalizing. Tentative *interpretation* of patterns. Positive and negative trends. Cite specifics that lead to your conclusion. Avoid accusations. Encourage exploration and elaboration. Relate to therapeutic goals.

Goals. Collaborate with client to develop and pursue objectives in harmony with client's wishes, values, and belief system. Substantial, legal and ethical.

Interpreting. Tentatively give your overall impres-sion of a pattern in the client's thoughts, feelings, and behaviors. *Generalizing*. Consider the cultural context.

Prompting. Similar to *furthering* to encourage the client to advance the story, but consists of *brief verbals* or nonverbal cues. "Go on." "And…?" Nod, curious expression, gesture, etc.

Redirecting. Bringing the session back on track when it gets too far off into unrelated subjects.

Resuming/Returning. *Directing* the session by picking up where it was previously left, either at the beginning or in reference to a salient point.

Specificity. When the client is too generalized, ask for more specific *clarification*. "Can you give me a few examples of what's happening there?"

Summarizing. Similar to *reflection* on a longer block of conversation or several sessions. Use tentative language like "typically," "usually," "tend to," "sounds like," "seems that," "there's a history of," rather than definitive language like "always" or "never."

Terminating. Progressively address feelings and thoughts about the finite nature of therapy. Review progress. Duration may be based on adequate resolution of issues or limited financial resources restricting the number of sessions. Recommend resources. Leave door open. Groups—ongoing or specific number of sessions, open/closed membership.

Transference. The client superimposes something from their past experience onto the therapist. Can be useful to help them deal with their issues.

Treatment Plan. Individualized rather than one size fits all. Young pedophiles are very different from adults. Exclusive attraction is not the same as a secondary attraction. Clarify roles and expectations. Prioritize collaborative goal for each session. Group therapy and/or private sessions? Will there be homework or assignments?

Impact Counseling

Visual illustrations of principles.

Empty Chair. "What would you say to your victim (or potential victim)?"

Magic Wand. "What do you wish your life would look like when we are done with therapy?"

Mobile. Represents the interrelatedness of the family system and what happens if you get out of balance.

Money. "How much is this ($5 bill) worth?" Crumple. Stomp it on the floor. Now how much is it worth? So you are still valuable.

Plate. Fill with good food. "You've got a plateful. Perhaps more than you can handle."

Rearview Mirror. "Sometimes it is necessary to

look back, but you can't move forward very well if you always look back."

Role-Playing. Psychodrama. Practice precise behavior patterns. Diagnostic: act out and discuss a situation. Behavioral experiment: practice alternative behaviors. Role swap: experience the impact of your behavior. Acquisition of coping strategies: practice problem solving. Some therapists use a life-size child doll.

Rubber Band (large). Have client hold it and then stretch it tight saying, "I'm going to let go of this and you won't get hurt." Release tension and then let go. Helps clients build trust in the process.

Motivational Interviewing

Express empathy. Roll with resistance. Develop discrepancy (between wishes and what is). Support self-efficacy. Avoid argumentation. Use change talk (benefits and hope of change, desire, ability, reasons, need, and commitment to change).

Change-Talk. Explore the problem (i.e., is it an addiction to pictures of children). Discuss dis-advantages (and advantages) of status quo. Discuss advantages (and disadvantages) of change. Encourage optimism about change. Affirm intention to change. Elaborate, summarize, and affirm change-talk. Clarify ambivalence between values and behavior. Discuss desire, ability, reasons, need, and commitment to change. Examine past experiences. Plan commitment to change. Set positive treatment goals.

Denial. Some clients may present for therapy under pressure of allegations of child sexual abuse which they deny or they may deny that they are sexually attracted to children. Therapy can sometimes be effective in spite of denial. See *roll with resistance*.

Develop Discrepancy. Dealing with stages of change. Contrast current behavior with goals and values to increase desire for change.

Express Empathy. Understand the client's feelings about their experience. Not sympathy or pity. Combine carefully with limited, generic self-disclosure. "I do understand what you are going through," only if you really understand. Honestly identify your own feelings. Avoid judgment and blame. Also include enhancing client's empathy for victims of CSA and client's potential victims.

Roll with Resistance. Don't fight it. See it as an indication of the need to change counseling approach. May be simple reflection, double-sided reflection, amplified (exaggerated) reflection, re-framing, or agreeing with a twist.

Ruler. "On a scale of 1 to 10, how confident are you about making this change?" Always ask why their confidence was not lower so they express strength toward change.

Support Self-Efficacy. Don't demand change.

Allow client to change at their own pace. Encourage client to engage in change-talk.

Suggestions for Clients

Belief. Encourage the client to believe in him/herself by believing in the client yourself. Irrespective of whether or not you believe in a higher power, encourage the client to utilize whatever spiritual support network they are comfortable with.

Castration. For those who inquire about it, inform the client about the benefits and downside of chemical or surgical castration. Testosterone blockers include Depo-Provera® and progesterone.

Cognitive Restructuring. Cognitive distortions and thinking errors are common among people with pedophilia, just as they are among other populations. Have the client *reframe* an alternative to what a child may be thinking when the pedophile thinks the child is coming on to them.

Coming Out. Discuss the pros and cons of the client disclosing his or her sexual orientation to a family member or friend. While coming out can provide a prevention partner, it can also backfire with rejection. If the client decides to come out, make sure you are available for support.

Disclosure. Make it safe to discuss difficult issues. If a client wants to talk about potential boundaries they may have violated, some therapists encourage them to phrase a situation in hypothetical terms or as a dream. Maintain genuine positive regard and nonjudgmental stance. Allow rather than demand.

Family support. Help client evaluate the strength of their family system, considering cautiously the possibility of *coming out* to select family members who might be able to handle the information.

Guilt. Internal feeling that one's emotions, lack of emotions, actions, inactions, or thoughts are unacceptable. Respect client's value system. Some people with pedophilia seek to avoid masturbating to fantasies involving children, while others find that it helps them avoid acting out with a real child.

Life Skills Training. Teach social skills emphasizing adult romantic and non-romantic relationships, as well as appropriate behavior with children. Model, role play, and demonstrate.

Medical Options. Even if you cannot prescribe, you should inform the client about SSRIs that often help with depression and have a side effect of lowering libido. Answer any questions about chemical castration. Provide a referral to a physician if needed.

Mindfulness. Method to cope with stress and undesirable feelings. Live in the moment by using all senses. Focus on a part of the body. Meditation. Yoga.

Relapse Prevention. Typical technique for offenders often dealing with the cycle of abuse that may not apply to non-offenders, although client may face a similar situation when tempted to abuse a child.

Safety Plan. Have the client identify his or her vulnerable situations, and develop a plan to protect children from being harmed and the client from false accusations.

Self-Control. Have the client identify a good habit they want to develop or a bad habit they want to break and help them develop self-control in that area of life. Discuss the effects of alcohol and other inhibition-reducing drugs.

Support Groups. Virtuous Pedophiles. 12-step programs (SA, SAA). Provides goal direction and positive social values from peers.

Vocational Training. Assess need. Develop work skills. Increase self-worth. Provide positive activities.

Suggestions for Therapists

Giving Advice. Use sparingly, preferably when requested. Identify the problem and the client's goal. Solicit possible solutions. Provide provisional options or strategies. Phrase responses as recommendations rather than demands. Base advice on comprehensive information of background, problems, goals, resources, beliefs, etc.

Informing. Answer a direct question. Educational information relevant to therapy. Correct misconceptions. Consider citing sources or expertise.

Matching. Match client's volume, tempo, tone, and sophistication of vocabulary, but don't be afraid to use accurate sexual words (such as masturbate instead of fap). Appropriate use of "neuro-linguistic programming."

Normalizing. Destigmatize the attraction without giving approval to act on it. Avoid the words "should," "ought," "right" or "wrong" when discussing attraction. Assure client that many people have a similar experience. Use research statistics.

Reframing. Propose an alternate positive interpretation of neutral or negative circumstances. Restating something the client has said about themselves with a more positive twist.

Self-Disclosure. Make sure you are comfortable sharing and that it is best for the client. Be authentic. Use sparingly. Avoid counter-transference or working on your own issues. Remember therapy is about the client, not the counselor.

Silence. Clients should be allowed to talk twice as much as the counselor. Become comfortable with a short pause, especially when something very sensitive has been shared. Time to think (client/counselor). Introspection. Encourage client to take responsibility. "Take your time." "You can start anywhere." "What do you want me to know?" "You seem (feeling word)." Not for brief therapy, initial session or crisis.

SOLER. **S**it straight facing the client (or perhaps a slight angle with female clients.) **O**pen posture; avoid crossing your arms or legs. Let hands rest naturally on lap. **L**ean forward occasionally but not in female client's space and not continuously. **E**ye contact. Look directly at the client's face without staring at them continuously. **R**elaxed demeanor.

Validation. Assure the client that his or her thoughts and feelings are appropriate for their unique situation and perspective. Acknowledge that it is difficult to ignore a sexual orientation. "Making friends with a child can be a lot easier than developing a relationship with an adult."

Value Judgments. Counselors are not to impose their values on clients, although clients should understand that you do not approve of any sexual interaction between an adult and a child.

Ask Questions. Preferably open-ended. May be phrased as a request. *Buffer*. One at a time. Avoid accusatory questions. Avoid "why" questions. Avoid multiple-choice. Avoid biased questions. Phrase non-judgmentally. Avoid implicit "right" answers.

Buffering. Include comments between questions so it does not seem like an interrogation. Avoid rapid-fire succession of questions.

Closed-Ended Questions. Limit use for specific information. If you do ask questions about CSA, they should be very specific. "Did you touch his penis?" rather than, "Did you ever abuse a child?"

Open-Ended Questions. Requires more than a "yes," "no," or one word answer. Broadly prompt storytelling. May be phrased as a request.

Repeating a Question. Rephrase or re-ask when client does not comprehend, it is so complex the client was unable to retrieve the answer, the client dodges because they feel judged or they dodge because it hurts (don't push too hard or force an answer).

Reverse Reflection. Respectfully request the client to restate what you said in their own words, to make sure the client really understood you.

Group Work

Blocking. Prevent inappropriate activities of any group member (gossiping, lengthy storytelling, breaking confidentiality).

Evaluating. Are group process and dynamics working? Includes member feedback.

Initiating. Provide structure and direction. Refocus on goals.

Linking. Connect group members, encouraging them to talk to each other in the group. Interactional. Suggest that clients join a peer-support group such as Virtuous Pedophiles. Caution group members about greeting each other in public places.

Modeling. Demonstrate desired behavior (risk taking, openness, directness, sensitivity, honesty, respect, enthusiasm). Co-leaders set norms.

Suggesting. More than advice. Tentative ideas for thinking or acting. Moderate member suggestions.

Supporting. Allow feelings to be therapeutic first. Being with a client in crisis (suicidal ideation or potential arrest). Clients can be resilient.

Not Recommended for Non-Offenders

Aversion therapy. Although it does not change a person's sexual orientation, some therapists still teach people with pedophilia to pair a bad odor (such as ammonia) with sexual fantasies involving children. Alternatives include thoughts of being arrested or snapping a rubber band on their wrist. This approach may provide some temporary modification of arousal patterns, but there is no evidence that it can change the kind of people that someone is attracted to. You should inform the client that this approach has been condemned for use with gay clients. Not recommended.

Plethysmograph. Volumetric or circumferencial penile test used to determine arousal patterns of offenders. Invasive and generally not appropriate for youth and non-offenders.

Polygraph. Test used forensically with offenders but is not recommended for non-offending pedophiles. Some therapists use it therapeutically to verify client honesty.

BIBLIOGRAPHY

Abel, G. & Harlow, N. (2001). *The Stop Child Molestation Book.* USA: Xlibris.

Ackerman, A., Harris, A., Levenson, J., & Zgoba, K. (2011). Who are the people in your neighborhood? A descriptive analysis of individuals on public sex offender registries. *International Journal of Law and Psychiatry 34* (2011) 149–159. Retrieved on May 3, 2012 from http://files.mail-list.com/m/atsa/0-Ackerman -et-al-2012-JofCJ-RSO-rates.pdf.

American Counseling Association (ACA, 2005). *ACA Code of Ethics*. Alexandria, VA: Author.

American Psychiatric Association (APA, 2013). *Diagnostic and Statistical Manual of Mental Disorders* (5th ed.). Arlington, VA: American Psychiatric Assoc.

American Psychological Association (APA, 2010). *Publication Manual of the American Psychological Association* (6th ed.). Washington, DC: Author.

American Psychological Association (APA, 2017). Guidelines for Affirmative Psychotherapy. Retrieved on 9/17/17 from http://www.apa.org/pi/lgbt/resources/guidelines.aspx.

Association for Sexual Abuse Prevention (ASAP 2015). Sexual Abuse Risk Assessment retrieved 9/17/15 from http://www.ASAPinternational.org.

Bailey, J. M., Hsu, K., & Bernhard, P. (2016). An internet study of men sexually attracted to children: Sexual attraction patterns. *Journal of Abnormal Psychology*, October 2016.

B4U-ACT (2011). Statement on Misinformation retrieved on 8/31/16 from http://www.b4uact.org/about-us/statements-and-policies/statement-about-misinformation.

B4U-ACT (2017). Psychotherapy for the Minor Attracted Person. Retrieved 9/17/17 from http://www .b4uact.org/gallery-2-columns-filter/psychotherapy-for-the-map/.

Beier, M., Neutze, J., Mundt, I. A., Ahlers, C. J., Goecker, D., Konrad, A., & Schaefer, G. E. (2009). Encouraging self-identified pedophiles and hebephiles to seek professional help: First results of the Prevention Project Dunkelfeld (PPD). *Child Abuse and Neglect, 33*(8), pp. 545–549.

Butcher, J. N., Mineka, S., & Hooley, J. M. (2012). *Abnormal Psychology* (14th ed.). Boston, MA: Pearson.

Cacciatori, H. (2017). *The lived experiences of men attracted to minors and their therapy-seeking behaviors.* (Unpublished doctoral dissertation). Walden University, Minneapolis, MN.

Cantor, J. M., & Blanchard, R. (2012). White matter volumes in pedophiles, hebephiles, and teleiophiles. *Archives of Sexual Behavior, 41, 749–752.*

Cantor, J. M., Blanchard, R., Christensen, B. K., Dickey, R., Klassen, P. E., Beckstead, A. L., Blak, T., & Kuban, M. E. (2004). Intelligence, memory, and handedness in pedophilia. *Neuropsychology, 18,* 3–14.

Cash, B. (2016). *Self-identifications, sexual development, and wellbeing in minor-attracted people: An exploratory study.* Unpublished manuscript. Department of Developmental Psychology, Cornell University, Ithaca, New York.

Chamberlain, L. L. (2013). Assessment and diagnosis. In Stevens, P., & Smith, R. L. (Eds.). *Substance Abuse Counseling: Theory and Practice* (5th ed.), pp. 122-154. Upper Saddle River, NJ: Pearson Education, Inc.

Crespi, T. D. (2009). Group counseling in the schools: Legal, ethical, and treatment issues in school practice. *Psychology in the Schools, 46*(3).

Dombert, B. & Schmidt, A. et al. (2016). How common is males' self-reported sexual interest in prepubescent children? *The Journal of Sex Research* 53, no. 2 (2016): 214-223.

Finkelhor, D. (2012). The National Center for Victims of Crime. Retrieved July 19, 2017 from http://victimsof crime.org/media/reporting-on-child-sexual-abuse/child-sexual-abuse-statistics.

Friedmond, C. (2013). *Navigating the stigma of pedophilia: The experiences of nine minor-attracted men in Canada*. Unpublished manuscript. Simon Fraser University, Burnaby, Canada.

Goode, Sarah D. (2010). *Understanding and Addressing Adult Sexual Attraction to Children: A Study of Paedophiles in Contemporary Society*. London, UK: Routledge.

Hall, G. C. N., Hirschman, R., & Oliver, L. L. (1995). Sexual arousal and arousability to pedophilic stimuli in a community sample of normal men. *Behavior Therapy, 26,* 681-694.

Hunter, S. V. (2006). Understanding the complexity of child sexual abuse: A review of the literature with implications for family counseling. *The Family*

Journal, *14*, 349–358.

Jespersen, A. F., Lalumiere, M. L, & Seto, M. C. (2009). Sexual abuse history among adult sex offenders and non-sex offenders: A meta-analysis. *Child Abuse & Neglect*, 33 (2009) 179-192.

Letourneau, E. (2017). Child sexual abuse in preventable, not inevitable. TEDMED talk. Retrieved 9/17/17 from http://tedmed.com/talks/show?id=620399.

McCutcheon, M. (1998). Roget's Super Thesaurus (second edition). Cincinnati, OH: Writer's Digest Books.

Namasté (2017). Retrieved 9/19/17 from https://www.namasteadvice.com/.

Prescott, David (Undated pdf). Retrieved 12/3/17 from http://www.unafei.or.jp/english/pdf/RS_No91/No91_10 VE_Prescott.pdf.

Remley, T. P., Jr., & Herlihy, B. (2010). *Ethical, Legal, and Professional Issues in Counseling* (3rd ed.). Upper Saddle River, NJ: Merrill/Pearson Education.

Rind, B., Tromovitch, P., & Bauserman, R. (1998). A meta-analytic examination of assumed properties of child sexual abuse using college samples. *Psychological Bulletin*, vol. 124, no. 1.

Santrock, J. W. (2009). *A Topical Approach to Life-Span Development* (custom ed.). New York: McGraw-

Hill.

Schmidt, W. E. (1983). Rape Sentence: Castration or 30 Years. *The New York Times*, Nov. 26, 1983.

Seto, M. (2008). *Pedophilia and Sexual Offending Against Children: Theory, Assessment, and Intervention.* Washington, DC, US: American Psychological Association.

Tabachnick, J. (2009). *Engaging Bystanders in Sexual Violence Prevention.* Enora, PA: National Sexual Violence Resource Center.

Tabachnick, J. & Klein, A. (2011). A reasoned approach: Reshaping sex offender policy to prevent child sexual abuse. Retrieved 7/8/11 from http://www.atsa.com/pdfs/ppReason-edApproach.pdf.

Ulrich, H., Randolph, M., & Acheson, S. (2005). Child Sexual Abuse: A replication of the meta-analytic examination of child sexual abuse by Rind, Tromovitch, and Bauserman (1998). *The Scientific Review of Mental Health Practice*, vol. 4, no. 2.

VirPed (2017). Retrieved on 12/9/17 from https://www.virped.org/f-a-q.html.

Webster, M. (2017). Merriam-Webster Learner's Dictionary. Retrieved 2/14/17 from http://www.learners dictionary.com/definition/pedophile.

Whiston, S. C. (2009). *Principles and Applications of*

Assessment in Counseling (3rd ed.). Belmont, CA: Brooks/Cole, Cengage Learning.

Wikipedia (2015). Retrieved on 1/12/15 from http://en.wikipedia.org/wiki/Westermarck_effect.

Wikipedia (2107a). Retrieved on 8/25/17 from https://en.wikipedia.org/wiki/Alcoholics_Anonymous.

Wikipedia (2017b). Retrieved 12/3/17 from https://en.wikipedia.org/wiki/Egosyntonic_and_egodyst onic.

Wortley, Richard K. (2015). Science and child sexual abuse: navigating the pathway between emotion and objectivity. *Crime Science* 2015, 4:1.

Zuckerman, E. L. (2008). *The Paper Office* (4th ed.). New York, NY: Guilford Press.

OTHER SUPPORTIVE ORGANIZATIONS

American Association for Sexuality Educators, Counselors and Therapists. https://www.aasect.org/.

Association for the Treatment of Sexual Abusers. http://www.atsa.com/.

B4U-ACT. Dialog among the mental health community and Minor Attracted Persons. http://www.b4uact.org/.

PedoHelp. Primary prevention treatment providers in France. https://pedo.help/.

Stop It Now. Primary prevention resources. http://www.stopitnow.org/.

StopSO. Primary prevention treatment providers in the UK. http://stopso.org.uk/.

Virtuous Pedophiles. Support group for people with pedophilia committed to not offending. http://virped.org/.

Additional copies of this book available from
Amazon.com

To contact the author:

GaryGibson7@yahoo.com
Phone 541-891-6168
www.ASAPinternational.org

Also recommended:
Untouchable: Reaching the Most Despised with God's Love
(2017) by Tabitha Abel

www.ingramcontent.com/pod-product-compliance
Lightning Source LLC
Chambersburg PA
CBHW051304250726
48656CB00004B/1474